That They Might Have Life

Through Christian Living

Megan McKenna

Benziger Publishing Company
Mission Hills, California

Cover Photographs:
Richard Hutchings; Jesus Washing St. Peter's Feet, Palatine Library, Parma, Italy/Erich Lessing, Culture and Fine Arts Archives/Photo Edit

Illustrations:
Titze Chao; Doug Paulin; Robert Phillips

Photographs:
Allan Oddie/Photo Edit 31, 70, 71, 83, 88, 142; Allsport/Steve Powell 121; Michael Amster 144; Art Resources 67; Marshall Berman 143; The Bettman Archive, Inc. 53, 81; C.A.R.E. 113; The Crosiers/Gene Plaisted 79, 85, 86, 130, 135, 146; Rohn Engh 41; Myrleen Ferguson/Photo Edit 9, 56; Bob Fletcher 116; Franciscan Communications 73; Peter Keegan 141; Stephen McBrady 17, 23, 55, 98, 102, 110, 125, 141; Megan McKenna 11, 87, 99; Photo Edit 16; Mark Richards/Photo Edit 43; Smith-Rowe 51, 65, 93, 107, 127; James Shaffer 30, 59, 100, 101; Steve Skjold/Photo Edit 27, 44, 45, 46, 72, 115; Bob Taylor 97; Anne Woehrle 96

Nihil Obstat:
Rev. Msgr. Joseph Pollard, S.T.D., V.F.
Censor Deputatus

Imprimatur:
†Roger M. Mahony
Archbishop of Los Angeles
November 1, 1987

The nihil obstat and imprimatur are official declarations that a book or pamphlet is free of doctrinal or moral error. No implication is contained therein that those who have granted the nihil obstat and imprimatur agree with the contents, opinions, or statements expressed.

Scripture passages are taken from the *New American Bible with Revised New Testament*. *Revised New Testament of the New American Bible*, copyright © 1986 by the Confraternity of Christian Doctrine, Washington, D.C. All rights reserved. *Old Testament of the New American Bible,* copyright ©1970 by the Confraternity of Christian Doctrine, Washington, D.C. All rights reserved.

Copyright © 1989 by Glencoe Publishing Company, a division of Macmillan, Inc. All rights reserved. No part of this book may be reproduced or transmitted in any form or by any means, electronic or mechanical, including photocopying, recording, or by any information storage and retrieval system, without permission in writing from the Publisher.

Send all inquiries to:
Benziger Publishing Company
15319 Chatsworth Street
Mission Hills, California 91345

Printed in the United States
ISBN 0-02-656270-7
  2 3 4 5 6 7 8 9   92 91 90

Contents

1	The First Three Commandments: I, the Lord, Am Your God	9
2	The Fourth Commandment: Honor Your Father and Your Mother	23
3	The Fifth Commandment: Respect Life	37
4	The Sixth and Ninth Commandments: Be Faithful and True	51
5	The Seventh and Tenth Commandments: Live Simply	65
6	The Eighth Commandment: Be Truthful	79
7	The Greatest Commandment: Love	93
8	The Beatitudes: Justice	107
9	The Beatitudes: Peace	121
10	Living in Christ Jesus	135

Introduction

Welcome to *That They Might Have Life*, a versatile worktext series, that is ideal for Youth Ministry groups. The activity oriented series also works well in CCD classes and many school situations because it allows a teacher or leader to match topics and exercises with the needs and abilities of the students.

This Introduction will describe the philosophy of the *That They Might Have Life* series and the content of its various components. You will be shown various options for using this series and will be given suggestions for implementing it under the model you choose.

The Philosophy of the Series

That They Might Have Life reflects the spirit and vision of the National Catechetical Directory, *Sharing the Light of Faith*, and the principles of youth ministry. There are four basic assumptions integral to the philosophy of this series:

1. Catechesis and the life of faith are related to human development which passes through stages or levels, recognizing that different people possess aspects of faith in varying degrees. The process of growth in faith is gradual and lifelong.
2. Catechesis and the life of faith involve a relationship, a friendship with persons. This involves "establishing and nurturing a real relationship to Jesus and the Father in the Holy Spirit, through a vigorous sacramental life, prayer, study and serving others" (*NCD*, 173).
3. Good catechesis always involves four essential elements: "koinonia" (community fellowship), "leitourgia" (shared faith in prayer and worship), "diakonia" (compassionate service), and "kerygma" (preaching and teaching). Through discussions and group activities, opportunities for community fellowship are provided. Suggestions for prayer are offered in many Scripture and group activities. Commitment to service through the integration of faith's tradition with one's life-style is encouraged in both the Scripture Activities and Group Activity. The Study sections provide sound biblical teaching respectful of the psychological and spiritual development of adolescents.
4. Principles of youth ministry recognize the importance of building community as foundational to more formal catechetical presentations. *That They Might Have Life* reflects this principle. The faith themes presented in *That They Might Have Life* are not designed to be academic courses, although they may be used as a resource for more academically focused programs. *That They Might Have Life* intends to facilitate growth in faith by presenting faith themes in the context of life experiences. *That They Might Have Life*'s approach is theologically incarnational—that is, its approach is guided by the recognition that Christ is present in the

events of daily existence. *That They Might Have Life* enables adolescents to discover Christ alive in them and in their world. Faith themes are presented to show how Scripture and Catholic teaching address the concerns of young people today.

The Components of the Series

Each title in the series is published in an 8½-by-11-inch worktext format that provides plenty of room for writing. Perforated, self-contained pages facilitate the convenient use of tear-out activities that students can work on at home, in a group, or privately.

The Old Testament: Topics covered in this worktext include how to read the Old Testament, creation, covenants with God, the prophets, sin and mercy, miracles, suffering and death, discipline and wisdom, prayer and love. Study aids include a timeline and a chart showing the categories into which the books fall.

The New Testament: This worktext contains chapters on how to read the New Testament, historical perspectives, the Gospels, the parables, the miracles, the Resurrection, Acts of the Apostles, the Epistles, and Revelation. A timeline and a chart categorizing the books are among the study aids.

The Sacraments: In this worktext there are individual chapters on the seven sacraments plus chapters that help students to understand Jesus' relationship to the sacraments and the role of the sacraments in the life of the Church.

Christian Living: This worktext presents the basic teachings of Christian morality through chapters on the Ten Commandments and the Beatitudes. With emphasis on the positive values of the commandments and of Jesus' teachings, the students are given a framework within which to make right moral decisions in their lives.

Discipleship: This worktext builds on the Christian Living text in order to bring the students to understand that living as a Christian is more a life-style and attitude than it is simply obeying rules. Topics covered include covenant, prophets, peace and justice, as well as a thorough treatment of Jesus' teachings as a basis for true Christian living.

Worktext Elements

Each of the worktexts is divided into topical chapters that relate to the main theme. Each chapter, in turn, is divided into five activities:

Preparation Activity: This section begins each chapter and is designed to prompt discussion and to begin the process of community building among the students.

Reading Activity: A short story centering on the theme presented in each chapter is designed to generate an emotional grasp of the topic. Think It Over questions at the end of each story enable the students to further explore and reflect on the main theme.

Study: This activity provides an overview of the subject matter in both an appealing style and appropriate vocabulary complexity which adolescents will find understandable. This section comprises the "kerygma" component of good catechesis. What About You questions at the end of this section help the students to see how the content of their faith relates to their own personal life situation.

Scripture Activities: Each chapter contains two Scripture activities. The catechist/facilitator can choose to use one or both of these. These activities give students the opportunity to work directly with the Bible and to become familiar with its various books.

Group Activity: This section is designed to help students to apply scriptural ideas to their own lives. If the Word does not become flesh in our own lives, then the Bible becomes mere history. These activities further develop a sense of community among the students and often lead to prayer or suggestions for service.

Options for Using the Series

There are three basic models for using the *That They Might Have Life* series: (1) Youth Ministry group meetings, (2) CCD classes, and (3) Catholic School quarter courses. In addition to these three models, this program can be used as a supplement to other programs that have a more academic focus. Each component can be used separately or together. Creativity on the part of the catechist/facilitator is encouraged.

Youth Ministry Meetings: Many teen groups tend to be flexible and open-ended. *That They Might Have Life* can benefit groups by providing activities that can be used to serve a number of different purposes. An organized format can be used similar to the one described under CCD Classes.

The Preparation Activity can be used as an ice-breaker for opening a youth group meeting.

Any of the elements of the program can be used separately as the needs of the group dictate.

A core group planning each youth group meeting can determine in advance which elements of the program will fit into the design of a particular session.

CCD Class Model: The more traditional parish high school CCD classes usually follow the principles of youth ministry which place a high value on community building and the integration of faith with life but prefer to establish learning situations within a formal catechetical structure. Often these classes are part of a larger, more comprehensive youth ministry effort in a parish community.

That They Might Have Life can be used in a variety of ways using the CCD classroom model. Each of the three components, the Old Testament, the New Testament, and the seven sacraments, can be divided into ten sessions each. These sessions can last from 60 to 90 minutes. Detailed lesson plans are provided in the Teacher's Manual. Each lesson plan is designed for a 60 minute class with optional steps suggested to extend the class an additional 30 minutes.

The creative catechist can spend more time on each element of the worktext, exploring each theme in greater depth, thus extending the classes to 20 sessions of a 60 minute duration or 30 sessions of a 45 minute duration.

The Catholic School Model: This model differs from the parish youth ministry and CCD models because of the frequency of classes. Instead of once-a-week formats, the typical Catholic School religion class meets four or five times each week. Good catechetical skills still recognize the importance of community building along with study.

That They Might Have Life may be used as a quarter elective with 30 sessions of 45 minutes. Each chapter could be extended over a three-day class period.

That They Might Have Life can also be used as a supplement to a more academically focused program. The Reading Activity, Scripture Activities, and Group Activity especially comprise material which the resourceful teacher can integrate into his or her lesson plan or assign as homework.

The School Model might also find this program helpful in designing campus ministry activities which place a high value on faith sharing.

The Catechist or Youth Minister's Role

1. Plan lessons in advance of the class.
2. Order books in advance.
3. Be aware of all lesson planning options.
4. Keep in mind the four essential elements of good catechesis: *community* building, faith sharing in *prayer* and *study*, invitation to *service*.
5. Possess an understanding, appreciation, and sensitivity to the psychological and spiritual development of adolescents.
6. Be a flexible "facilitator" of faith growth.
7. Keep in mind that it is essential for faith that the Word become flesh in the lives of your students!

1 The First Three Commandments:
I, the Lord, Am Your God

PREPARATION PAGE

Obedience and Morality

1. Whom do you obey? Make a list of them.

   _____
   _____
   _____
   _____
   _____

2. Why do you usually obey them?

   _____
   _____
   _____
   _____
   _____

3. If you were to lose everything in the world that you treasure, what would you hold onto until the very end? Why?

   _____
   _____
   _____
   _____
   _____
   _____

READING ACTIVITY

Saint of Conscience

Sir Thomas More was beheaded at the Tower Hill in London on July 6, 1535, in the twenty-seventh year of the reign of King Henry the Eighth. He was executed for refusing to sign an oath written by King Henry that approved the king's disobedience to the laws of the Church. King Henry had divorced his first wife and was seeking to marry again, claiming that, as king, he was entitled to change the laws. Sir Thomas More was the only one among the heads of state and advisors to the king who refused to sign the oath or give a reason why he refused. He placed the demands of his conscience and his obedience to God above his obedience to the king of England.

Thomas More struggled with his responsibilities to God, to his king, to his family, and to his own conscience. The play, *A Man For All Seasons,* by Robert Bolt, depicts what it was that drove More to be silent and to refuse the king's oath and thereby face his own death. Sir Thomas learned that his deeds, his words, and his very silence were on behalf of others, and he paid a stiff price for his beliefs. Margaret, his daughter, attempted to "reason" with him:

Margaret: In any country that was half good, you would already be raised on high.
Thomas: If we lived in a country where virtue was profitable, common sense and reason would make us good. And good would make us saints.
Margaret: But in reason! Haven't you done as much as God could reasonably want?
Thomas: Well . . . finally . . . it isn't a matter of reason. Finally, it is a matter of love.

Saint Thomas More lived in a time that called for ethical decisions and choices that put the souls and bodies of men and women in jeopardy. He used all of his learning and knowledge to stay alive and all of his craft and politics to outwit the king; but in the end there was only once choice: whether or not to obey the first three commandments of God. "I, the Lord, am your God . . . . You shall not have other gods beside me . . . . You shall not bow down before them or worship them. For I, the Lord, your God, am a jealous God . . . . You shall not take the name of the Lord, your God, in vain . . . . Remember to keep holy the sabbath day" (Exodus 20:2–8). Thomas obeyed God and lost his life, but he retained his honor, his human dignity, and his soul.

Thomas More respected the law, both God's law and that of the state, and he recognized the demands and priorities of each.

The law, for Thomas More, was his safety, his boundary, his guide for conduct, and his hope for his life. Obedience to the law was right living. It defined his relationships with others, his king, and his God. Obedience situated him in society and told him how to live as a human being. The laws of the Church and the Ten Commandments told him how to live as a Christian, a believer in Jesus. His relationship to God came first in his life—over and above his relationship with the king and the state. He knew whom to obey and who had the stronger hold on him, despite the consequences of disobeying the one to obey the other. God's way was the guiding principle of More's life, and as long as the laws of the land served the laws of God, he followed and obeyed them. But when the laws of the state broke the laws of God, More chose not to obey, and he suffered the price of his choice. Sir Thomas More believed in and followed one God, the God of the Old Testament, Yahweh, and Jesus' God, called Father. He would bow to no other god or law, even if it meant losing all he had struggled for, worked for, and achieved.

Sir Thomas More is sometimes called the "saint of conscience" because his conscience led him to disregard one set of laws and authority for the obedience of God, who is the first authority. His conscience and his obedience to God's law cost him his life. Thomas More was beheaded for publicly going against the king's decree and saying with his life that God's law was the law upon which all other laws were based. He followed his conscience in love, trying to explain his position to his family, friends, and members of the state, none of whom believed that his dedication to the law was worth his life. But for Thomas More, it was worth more than his life. It was worth his soul.

THINK IT OVER

1. Do you agree with Margaret, Thomas More's daughter, that God only expects us to do what is reasonable? If so what would reason say to do in order to save your life?
2. What does Thomas More mean when he says, "Finally, it is not a question of reason, but of love"?
3. What is the difference between loving and obeying someone?

STUDY

Laws: The Signatures of God

When Moses is given the Law in the Book of Exodus and comes down the mountain, he sees the people below him dancing and worshiping the golden calf. These people have already broken the first of the commandments of Yahweh, and so Moses breaks the tablets of the Law, the Ten Commandments of God to his people. The tablets of the Law were holy, not because of what was written on them, but because of *who* wrote them and for whom they were written. They are the signatures of God. They are God-given, full of power and holiness.

And so, in chapter 19 of the Book of Leviticus, after each of the commandments, there are the words: "I am the Lord." The power and the meaning of the Law comes from the giver. For someone who believes in God, there is no such thing as autonomous ethics and morality apart from faith. To make or create laws in opposition to the law of God is to create an idol.

Social conscience, individual reasoning, and the laws of any country or group are not enough to keep us from evil. God is the *only* reason why we do good, make choices, and consciously avoid evil. In Matthew's Gospel, when Jesus is approached by a lawyer, he is called "Good teacher." Jesus responds, "No one is good but God alone." Our criteria for good are based on God's actions toward us and our response to him as our God.

Belief in God is the basis of all ethics and morality. To believe involves words, actions, life-style, and attitudes; to believe encompasses our mind, heart, body, and soul. We begin to believe and to live that belief with the laws of God, and as Christians, we grow into the depth of the Law's spirit with Jesus' understanding of what is God's will for all people. This is called the new law of love: You shall love the Lord your God with all your heart and all your mind and all your soul and all your strength and your neighbor in the same way. As a believer in Jesus Christ as our Lord, as the brothers and sisters of Jesus, we obey God as Jesus obeyed him, "obedient to death, even death on a cross" (Philippians 2:8).

> *There is no such thing as autonomous ethics.*

The Image of God

As human beings, we are first bound and related to God. The book of our beginnings, Genesis, tells us: "God created man in his image: in the divine image he created him; male and female he created them." We are born to be like God, to relate to one another as God relates to us, to choose and to act as God chooses and acts. And God is life. When Moses asks God who he should say sent him to the people, God replies "I AM"—life, existence, being. And when Joshua sets the Law given to Moses by God before the people, he asks them, "Do you choose this day, life or death?" For one who believes in God, all morality depends on life, on God and his commandments, and on his word. The law of the Ten Commandments is where we begin, with "Thou shalt not." But for a believer, it is just as important to bring life, affirm life, choose life, and be life for others—in imitation of God. And so our study of morality begins with the Ten Commandments, but there will be more emphasis on what is right and just and positive in the commandments, and not just the negative. For if God is our primary reason for living, then *not* to do something isn't enough on which to build a relationship.

Living in the Spirit of God's Laws

The first three commandments call us to obey God first and foremost: to be devoted to God, his will, his kingdom, and his rule over us, and to put all of our energies—body and soul—and lives into obeying his laws. These commandments call us not to use the name of God in vain by wasting it or using it for our own purposes, carelessly or dishonestly. They call us instead to worship, to keep holy a day unto the Lord, to let nothing else—job, money, possessions, prestige, reputation—get in the way of our primary relationship, of belonging to God alone.

These commandments remind us to honor God. The other seven commandments are built on our relationship to God; if we only half-heartedly believe in and honor God, then the other commandments will carry no power or weight. And if we call ourselves Christians, then our relationship to Jesus as our Lord calls us to live in the spirit of the Law. We are invited to worship and live like Jesus:

> Come to me, all you who labor and are burdened, and I will give you rest. Take my yoke upon you and learn from me, for I am meek and humble of heart; and you will find rest for yourselves. For my yoke is easy, and my burden light.
>
> Matthew 11:28–30

For those who follow Jesus and take his yoke upon them, the way will be easy, the meaning will be clear, and the burden will be light because Jesus has already gone before us. But our beginning choice is to believe in God, in Jesus Christ our Lord, and in his Spirit given to us as the truth, judgment, and protector of our lives.

Our Jewish Roots

As Christians we are really Jews first, just as Jesus was a Jew. Throughout the Scriptures we are told that Jewish people lived by their word. They took their religion, their belief, and their obedience to God very seriously. They freely chose the life of God as their life, publicly proclaiming that God, Yahweh, was the one God. Their lives reflected his care for them and his presence with them. The Book of Exodus tells the story of God's deliverance of the Israelites from bondage in Egypt and his journey with them, through the Red Sea and the desert, into the land of promise. At the Mount of Sinai, he made them his people and gave them his laws through Moses.

They had seen his glory and knew that he had saved them from slavery and death. God's words—delivered to them through Moses—were clear:

> "Thus shall you say to the house of Jacob; tell the Israelites: You have seen for yourselves how I treated the Egyptians and how I bore you up on eagle wings and brought you here to myself. Therefore, if you hearken to my voice and keep my covenant, you shall be my special possession, dearer to me than all other people, though all the earth is mine. You shall be to me a kingdom of priests, a holy nation. That is what you must tell the Israelites." So Moses went and summoned the elders of the people. When he set before them all that the Lord had ordered him to tell them, the people all answered together, "Everything the Lord has said, we will do." Then Moses brought back to the Lord the response of the people.
>
> Exodus 19:3–8

The people's relationship with God was sealed in a covenant, a promised obedience to God's laws, in return for which God would be faithful to them and they would be God's own people. Their obedience to his laws would reveal to all other nations that he was their God. They would show forth God's glory so that all the earth could see that God was with them. The first three commandments revealed that they believed in and worshiped only one God, and the last seven commandments revealed that their God called them to treat one another with respect and dignity as his people.

The Friends of Jesus

The books of the Old Testament contain the stories of God and his people, their faithfulness and obedience to his commandments, as well as their unfaithfulness and disobedience. They were made a great nation and promised a Messiah, someone who would be so just, true, and merciful that he would be the presence of God within them and they would recognize him as the peace and justice of God. The prophets called the people back to their word of honor and their way of living as God's own people.

It is Jesus who is the long-awaited one, the Messiah who is holy and just. Jesus is the fulfillment of the old Law and covenant with God and his people. Jesus clearly reveals the values of God for all to see. The first value of Jesus is conversion, turning to God the Father by following the way of Jesus. Christians begin by turning away from all that is not true to Jesus' values, continually turning to follow Jesus' ways more closely. This conversion, this obedience to Jesus' values and commandments, reveals a relationship with God our Father so that others know who we worship and what our God is like. We are known as Christians by our actions, attitudes, and obedience to the new commandments, the new laws Jesus brings to those who will believe in him and follow him as the Way, the Truth, and the Life. In John's Gospel, at the Last Supper, Jesus tells his disciples about God's new relationship with them:

As the Father loves me, so I also love you. Remain in my love. If you keep my commandments, you will remain in my love, just as I have kept my Father's commandments and remain in his love. I have told you this so that my joy might be in you and your joy might be complete. This is my commandment: love one another as I love you. No one has greater love than this, to lay down one's life for one's friends. You are my friends if you do what I command you. I no longer call you slaves, because a slave does not know what his master is doing. I have called you friends, because I have told you everything I have heard from my Father. It was not you who chose me, but I who chose you and appointed you to go and bear fruit that will remain, so that whatever you ask the Father in my name he may give you. This I command you: love one another.

John 15:9–17

Laws as the Sign of Unity

Just as the laws of the old covenant, the Ten Commandments, held the Israelites together and made them the People of God, so the laws of the new covenant, Jesus' commandments, hold his followers together and make us his people. We are his disciples, protecting what Jesus believed in and preached. The person of Jesus gives authority and meaning to his commandments. We obey these commandments because we believe that God the Father loves us and that this is how we can reflect God in our lives. This is why we reflect Jesus to others, so that they can see our belief. We are the friends of God, the People of God, his Church—*if* we obey his commandments of love and forgiveness. People will know that we are Christians by observing how we love and relate to one another, just as Christians were recognized in the early Church. If we do not obey, others cannot see that Jesus has power and meaning in our lives.

Disobedience to the Laws of Love

Although we profess to believe in Jesus as Lord of our lives and to follow his commandments as children of the Father, we often fail and do not live up to our words. We disobey, we fail, and we sin. To sin means to miss the mark. The commandments and values of Jesus are the marks of Christian life. When we do not live up to the values of Jesus and deliberately choose other values, then we miss the mark and commit sin. The process of becoming a Christian only *begins* with Baptism, with our acceptance of being a follower of Jesus, and it continues all of our lives. At each step of our life we are asked to recommit ourselves to following Jesus and obeying his commandments. We grow in understanding of what it means to be disciples. We begin with the Ten Commandments of the Old Testament, and then we grow into the further demands and expectations of the new law of love and the Beatitudes of Jesus. All the commandments and laws, however, are based on love of Jesus as well as love and worship of God as our Father, who calls us to be his children, giving him glory and honor by our lives.

The new commandment is simple and all encompassing: "You shall love the Lord your God with all your heart and all your soul and all your mind and all your strength, and you shall love your neighbor as yourself." Sometimes it makes the second half of the commandment clearer if you read it as you do the first: "and you shall love your neighbor with all your heart and all your soul and all your mind and all your strength." As disciples, we try to love God and one another by emulating the intensity and care with which God has loved us.

We each have an individual relationship with God through our faith and our baptism. But each of us is also related to one another. We call God our Father, and so we are brothers and sisters to one another. Jesus is our elder brother, who shows us how to live and to love one another. In Baptism, we are given a gift of God, the Holy

To sin means to miss the mark.

Spirit, the Spirit of Jesus, to strengthen and encourage us to be true disciples. We are baptized into a community of followers, the Church, the community that lives out the faith of Jesus, incorporating the values of Jesus into its life in the world. This community supports us, teaches us all we need to know, makes us disciples, and sends us out into the world to stand up for what we believe. We are called to proclaim the goodness of God to others. The Church helps us to mature and grow to become adult children of God through the Scriptures, the sacraments, prayer and liturgy, as well as through sharing life in community.

Whenever we fail to live as followers of Jesus, we betray our belief in God our Father, Jesus our Brother, and the Spirit that is given to us, and we betray our participation in the community that believes in Jesus. Our individual lives either contribute to the life force of the Church or make it more difficult for others to believe in Jesus and to live as his followers. Sin—missing the mark that has been set for us by Jesus—has both individual and collective effects. Our failures are never purely personal; they always affect others who are part of our Church community. But it is also our sins and our failures that teaches us the depth of the values that we have accepted as Christians.

> *Our failures are never purely personal; they always affect others who are part of our Church community.*

The Challenge of Jesus

This course is a study of morality—right living as a follower of Jesus Christ. Morals reveal our discernment between right and wrong, between good and evil. Morals reveal our standards and our principles of belief and action. Christian morality, the morals of Jesus, is a challenge to anyone who wishes to live honestly, worshiping God as Jesus did. Jesus challenges us to follow him, to imitate him, to obey him, and to love as he loved. Jesus presents us with moral imperatives. In the desert, the Israelites were challenged to choose life or to choose death. As Christians, we are challenged to choose life over death, life with love, love unto death. For Christians, there is always more to choose because Jesus brings life everlasting and shares that with us now. We are challenged to follow him more closely, love him more dearly, and imitate him more nearly. It is a lifelong commitment to change, to turn and follow Jesus alone, to obey God first and foremost, as Saint Thomas More did, even if it means losing one's life.

WHAT ABOUT YOU?

1. What names do you use for God?
2. What does each of those names say about your relationship to God?
3. Are you willing to accept the word/law of God as the reason for your moral choices, decisions, and actions? What is hard about that acceptance? What makes it easy or possible to say yes?

SCRIPTURE ACTIVITY

Jesus Obeys God

Look up the following Scripture passages to see how Jesus obeys God and what he says about our primary relationship to God.

SCRIPTURE	JESUS' OBEDIENCE	OUR RELATION TO GOD
John 5:19		
John 8:49b–50		
Matthew 5:33–37		
Matthew 5:17–20		
John 3:36		
John 4:34		

SCRIPTURE ACTIVITY

True Authority Comes from God

Read John 18:18–19:11, the story of Jesus as he was brought before Pilate and questioned. Answer the following questions:

1. Who does Pilate say Jesus is?

2. Who does Jesus say he is?

3. What kind of power does Pilate have?

4. Where does Jesus say that power comes from?

5. What is the relationship between Jesus and Pilate as you see it?

GROUP ACTIVITY

Standing Up for Your Beliefs and Values

Situation: A new government comes into power in the United States. One of its first laws is that all citizens, under penalty of imprisonment and fine, are required to work on Sundays because the economic health of the country is most important. Anyone caught worshiping instead of working will be fined the first time, fired from their job the second time, and imprisoned for the third offense.

Answer the following questions:

1. What could your parish do to ease the burden of individuals having to choose between work and worship?

   _____
   _____
   _____
   _____

2. What could your parish do to protest the law?

   _____
   _____
   _____
   _____

3. What would your reasons be for your own actions?

   _____
   _____
   _____
   _____
   _____

Write a petition to the government to change the law. Use the outline to work out the details of the petition.

NAME OF PARISH/CHURCH: _____

THE LAW AND ITS PENALTIES: _____

WHY THE LAW UNJUST OR UNFAIR: _____

PROPOSED ALTERNATIVES (to help the economy): _____

WHOSE AUTHORITY YOU OBEY AND WHY: _____

PETITION

WHEREAS we, _____ , feel that

2 The Fourth Commandment:
Honor Your Father and Your Mother

PREPARATION PAGE

Family Ties

1. What do you think is the strongest human relationship? Why?

2. What gifts have you received from your parents and grandparents?

3. Who do you include in your family? Why do you relate to them differently than to others?

READING ACTIVITY

The Merit of a Young Priest

It was June, 1942. The murder of Jews in the Cracow ghetto was at its height. About five thousand victims were deported to the Belzec death camp. The Hiller family realized that their days in the ghetto were numbered and they worried about their son. They were strong, but he couldn't survive. Helen and Moses Hiller began to plan the rescue of their child Shachne. They decided to contact Gentile friends, a couple named Yachowitch, who lived in the small town of Dombrowa.

With the help of the Jewish underground, Helen made her way to Dombrowa and begged the Yachowitch family to take care of her son. Although they could do so only at great risk to their own lives, the Christian friends agreed to take Shachne. On November 15, 1942, Helen Hiller smuggled her child out of the ghetto. Along with her son, she gave her Christian friends two envelopes. One contained all the Hillers' valuables; the other, letters and a will. One of the letters was addressed to Mr. and Mrs. Yachowitch, entrusting them with Shachne and asking them to raise the child as a Jew and to return him to his people in case of his parents' death. The letter also included the names and addresses of relatives in Montreal, Canada and Washington, D.C. The second letter was written to Shachne, expressing how much his parents loved him and explaining how this love had prompted them to leave him alone with strangers, who were good and noble people. In the letter they told him of his Jewishness and how they hoped that he would grow up to be a man who would be proud of his Jewish heritage. A third letter was addressed to Helen's sister-in-law, Jenny Berger, in Washington, D.C., and it contained a will. It asked Jenny to take the child if the Hillers did not return, to raise the child righteously, and to reward Mr. and Mrs. Joseph Yackowitch. More than anything else, the Hillers wanted their child to grow up a Jew.

Eventually, the Yachowitchs found out that the Hillers were dead. Afraid that their neighbors would turn them in, they, too, began to move around and to stay out of the way of the Gestapo. Mrs. Yachowitch was a devout Catholic. She grew attached to Shachne and began taking him to church and then she decided to have the child baptized. She went to a young parish priest who had a reputation for being wise and trustworthy, and she revealed the secret identity of the little boy. The priest listened attentively to the woman's story and then asked her what the parents' wish was in entrusting the child to her. Mrs. Yachowitch told the priest about the letters and the mother's last request that her child be raised Jewish and returned to his people in the event of the parents' death. The priest explained that it would be unfair to baptize the child, and he did not perform the ceremony. That was in 1946.

Some time later, Mrs. Yachowitch mailed the letters to Jenny Berger in Washington, D.C., and to relatives in Montreal. The family immediately responded and said they'd be delighted to raise Shachne in the States. For four years, however, legal battles kept Shachne in Poland. Finally, in 1949, the child was brought to Canada. Leaving Mrs. Yachowitch was painful for Shachne, but she comforted him by reminding him of his mother's wish and hope for him. Finally, in 1951, Shachne arrived in the United States, more than eight years since his parents had given him up in the hope of his life being spared.

Shachne grew up to be an observant Jew, the vice-president of a company, well educated, and concerned about others who were caught in the same situation during the war. In 1978, Mrs. Yachowitch, with whom he had kept in contact by letter, finally told him of her plan to baptize him a Catholic. She described her meeting with the newly ordained priest and how he had refused to perform the ceremony. That parish priest, in fact, was Cardinal Karol Wojtyla of Cracow. On October 16, 1978, he had been elected Pope John Paul II.

When the rabbi of Bluzhov heard this story, he commented: "God has mysterious, wonderful ways unknown to men. Perhaps it was the merit of saving a single Jewish soul that brought about his election as Pope. It is a story that must be told."

THINK IT OVER

1. What decisions that were made by Mr. and Mrs. Yachowitch were crucial for the Jewish boy? Why do you think they made them?
2. Did the young priest's refusal to baptize the child surprise you? What did you think he would do?
3. Are there any similarities between your family and the Hiller family?

STUDY

Honor in the Family

The fourth commandment of God to his people is: "Honor your father and your mother that you may have a long life in the land which the Lord, your God is giving you." This commandment is the basis of our relationship with our family and with all of our blood relatives and relations by marriage: sisters, brothers, aunts, uncles, and cousins. Our God is the God of life, and those who give us life imitate God. That is why we owe them obedience, care, respect, and honor—just as we do to God.

What does it mean to honor? The dictionary says it is to hold in high regard, to respect, to give glory, to adhere to principles considered right, to have integrity, to defer to rank or distinction, something done or given as a token of gratitude or respect, to accept and take care of, and to be chaste toward someone or something. These are all the positive values of the commandment. Again, it is the quality of one's relationship to God and the depth of one's worship that will effect the quality and depth of the honor given to one's family.

Our families give us histories, memories, culture, a story, life, a childhood, education, relationships, roots, and possibilities—both positive and negative. Jesus' own family did the same for him. Mary and Joseph, in their response to God, reveal many of the decisions and actions that this commandment asks of us. In the Incarnation (God becoming human, one of us), Mary says yes to life, in the face of danger. To be found pregnant while still betrothed meant that she would be stoned to death. Joseph also accepts and adopts the child of God and raises him as his own, taking Mary as his wife, even though he knows the child is not his. Both Mary and Joseph struggle in dangerous historical circumstances to give the child life and to protect him from harm. They are even willing to go into exile, as "illegal aliens" in Egypt. When they return to Palestine, they choose to live in Nazareth, a place "nothing good comes from," because it is the last place that Herod will think to look for the child. The safety and the life of the child is the basis of their decision making. Their own love for each other and for God gives them the courage to do what is necessary. And all the while we are told that Mary "treasured all these things in her heart." She wondered, prayed, and struggled to obey.

Jesus, too, is described as living out the positive demands of this commandment: "He went down with them and came to Nazareth, and was obedient to them; and his mother meanwhile kept all these things in her heart. And Jesus advanced in wisdom and age and favor before God and man" (Luke 2:51–52).

Jesus grew in wisdom and age and favor before God and man.

The Family of Jesus

Because of his obedience to this commandment, Jesus remained at home until he was thirty years old. A widow in Jewish society had only one right: if her husband died, she was to marry his brother; if her husband had no brother, her firstborn son was to care for her until he was thirty years old.

The relationship of Jesus to his parents is unknown in detail. But when Jesus is teaching in public and someone informs him that his mother and brothers are standing outside and want to speak with him, he replies:

> "Who is my mother? Who are my brothers?" And stretching out his hand toward his disciples, he said, "Here are my mother and my brothers. For whoever does the will of my heavenly Father is my brother, and sister, and mother."
>
> Matthew 12:48–50

All those who give us life in God become our family. All those with whom we share Baptism and Eucharist become our family. We call ourselves the sons and daughters of God, the brothers and sisters of Jesus. God is our Parent; we are his children. In our families, we are introduced to life, to living with one another, to loving, rejoicing, and suffering. What is demanded of us in relation to our families—respect, care, concern, honesty, privacy, protection, and returning the favor to our parents in their old age—is where to begin to practice what Jesus preaches that we must do to all people. In Matthew 25, Jesus clearly says that what is done to the least of our brothers and sisters is done to him, and what we neglect to do for them, we neglect to do for him. Our families are our first relationships where we are to practice the works of mercy, forgiveness, and simple human kindness. The old adage, "Charity begins at home," is true.

Love Begins at Home

We all begin as children, with a family that gives us our first look at the world and helps us to develop a sense of who we are in that world. And each of us, as Christians, calls God our Father. Our first promise in Baptism states that we promise to live as the children of God. In Mark's Gospel, we see Jesus blessing the children:

> People were bringing children to him that he might touch them, but the disciples rebuked them. When Jesus saw this he became indignant and said to them, "Let the children come to me; do not prevent them, for the kingdom of God belongs to such as these. Amen, I say to you, whoever does not accept the kingdom of God like a child will not enter it." Then he embraced them and blessed them, placing his hands on them.
>
> Mark 10:13–16

We are the children of God at every age. God blesses us and cares for us both in the family into which we are born and in the family of his followers, the Church. It is here that we grow up, discovering what it means to be sons and daughters of God and

God blesses us and cares for us both in the family into which we are born and in the family of his followers, the Church.

brothers and sisters to one another. We initially practice the values of this love with our mother and father and siblings. What we learn to treasure and honor among our blood ties is then extended to others. Our biological families are the homes that nurture us and begin our lives, setting the basis and the foundation for our images of ourselves as children of God. Our parents introduce us to the concept of mothering and fathering, of trust and care, of love and forgiveness.

The Right to Life

The most basic value of a believer is that of life: life for all, abundant life, as Jesus promised his disciples. The primary value protected by the fourth commandment is that of existence. This commandment calls us to look at the treasured gift of creation, of love that creates and is brought forth in the person of a child, conceived in response to both God's commandment and two people's love for each other. God creates and gives life, and we imitate God and share in his creativity when we conceive and bring forth children. As we continue his act of creation, our own love continues for all to see. The gift of procreation and the extension of love is the basis of the family. The nurturing of life in the family from birth to death is one of the values of this commandment: to honor our father and mother so that we may have a long life in the land. The honor that belongs to human life is protected and given possibility in the family. The protection of life and of children is based on worshiping the God of life.

Health and Life in Abundance

The quality of life in a family and home reveals the beliefs and values of that family. We honor God by the honor and respect we give to one another; the abuses of life and health and persons in the family are positively prohibited by this commandment. The sins of abuse—whether sexual, physical, psychological, or chemical—are condemned as destructive and are in direct opposition to the respect demanded by this commandment. It is in the family that the quality of life, health, and happiness is nurtured. Any behavior that disrespects the bonds of mother and child, father and child, or brother and sister destroys the family and creates dysfunctional relationships that must be dealt with throughout life. We are called to cherish and deal with one another with dignity, privacy, and care, and not to abuse the closeness of relationships within our families. Any family that experiences the brokenness and destructiveness of abuse needs to seek help, counseling, and support from the Church and medical communities.

Long Life in the Land

Lastly, this commandment reminds us of the promise of life, health, happiness, and generativity. Old age, maturity, and seeing our children's children to the third and fourth generation have always been considered blessings from God. This bonding of family extends to aging parents and grandparents as well. Our response to our elderly family members reveals whether or not we return the favor of nurturing life that was once afforded to us when we were young. The care of the old, the infirm, and the senile is protected and encouraged by this commandment as gestures of tendering life.

If God truly controls our lives and if our living comes from his power and goodness, then we must make sure that all people's lives are cared for and that they experience this goodness of creation while they are alive. Human life is not equal, but we are called especially to watch out for and give a chance to life that is struggling. This is not a question of the survival of the fittest, but the graceful survival of all who live. We are required to do all that is necessary to prolong life. Our Christian morality demands that we protect life and not allow others to die because we feel sorry for them or are tired of caring for them or because they have become a burden to us.

Family Life

Each family is unique. Whether we grow up in a family with only one child or in a family of twelve, these people we are born to or adopted by either give us a headstart on life or make it difficult for us to grow and love as adults. Jesus was an only child, but he called his disciples to treat one another as brothers and sisters in his love. The qualities of kindness, care, courtesy, compassion, openness, honesty, truthfulness, reliance, trustworthiness, devotion, and loyalty are basic to good family relations. The old adage "the family that prays together stays together" is true, but it is founded on an even more basic premise. The family that talks and listens to one another can pray and grow in affection together.

Just as we are known and singled out by our names, by our relatives, and by the unique characteristics of our families, so we are singled out as believers and known by the company we keep in the world. The Church protects the values and lives of all people, calling them brothers and sisters and treating them as children of God. We are family. The care of human life begins in our immediate families, but the church extends that care to all who are bound to us by water in Baptism and by need in the world. As Catholics, we are to stand up for and protect all life, from birth until death, and to help ensure that all people live with health, human dignity, possibility, freedom, and simple human kindness. The quality of life is continually growing, and there are always ways to enhance life and enrich human relationships with one another. This fourth commandment is the cornerstone for valuing life. All the other commandments will build on the basic necessities that are set forth here.

Authority and Life

The story of Pope John Paul II when he was a young priest reveals another aspect of this commandment: the need to respect authority. Certain people, by reason of their very way of existing, call us to honor and respect them. Although all people deserve respect and acknowledgment of their persons as human beings, some people—by reason of their age, wisdom, gifts, and vested authority—command our respect in specific ways. All authority comes from God, and we obey any authority because of its relationship to God. As human beings we acknowledge laws: those of our families (usually unwritten but understood by each member), of the state and local governments, of the nation, of the world, and of the Church. Each group to which we belong teaches us to conform our behavior and to respect the values the laws protect. In return for obedience to the law, we are afforded privileges, acceptance, and protection of our persons. To break the law is to incur penalty, whether we are caught speeding by the police or sneaking in late at night by a parent.

There are persons in authority over us. When they remind us of the laws and call us to protect our values and to live up to our beliefs, we must afford them respect. No one wants to be reminded of failure or to have mistakes pointed out or to be accused, even justly, of not being truthful about what we proclaim and what we do. It is the role and duty of the person in authority to call us to live up to our beliefs and dignity as human persons. Within the Church there are those in authority who should be listened to and not casually ignored in the areas of obedience.

The Pope is the teacher, defender, and protector of the values of the Church, especially in cases where the world would like to forget or change those values concerning human life. The Church is called and commissioned by God to remember and expressly care for those whom society does not want to care for or is quick to forget and let die. It is the responsibility of the Church, its leaders and *all* its members, to publicly defend human life—from conception, through all of its years and growth, until it is finished gracefully. The Church has both the right and the responsibility to question and to give guidelines on how all life is to be conceived, nurtured, sustained, and protected. This pattern of Christian morality has recently been called the "seamless garment" of life. In future chapters it will be studied in more detail and specifics. For the present, the issue of authority and the respect due to those who stand and witness for life in all forms is part of the call of this commandment.

The God of the Living

"We are part and parcel of the whole world and cannot find God apart from the rest of humanity." This quotation from the nonviolent prophet of India, Mahatma Gandhi, reminds us of our common bond as family in the world. In the Old Testament, there were prophets who called the people of Israel to account for their belief and their faith. They preached the God of life, of justice, and of mercy. Today we also have prophets who preach the God of life and hope for all peoples and who call us to live out our belief in practice, especially in defense of life. The fourth commandment calls us to begin where we live and where we were born to make the world a truly human family for all. As Mother Teresa wisely said, "Love begins at home."

We are part and parcel of the whole world and cannot find God apart from the rest of humanity.

WHAT ABOUT YOU?

1. How does your family help you to obey the commandments of God? Be specific and provide examples.
2. How can family members make it difficult to obey God?
3. Have you thought about your responsibility to your parents in terms of returning to God the life he has shared with you through them? How can you begin to be thankful for that life?

SCRIPTURE ACTIVITY

Who Is My Mother, Brother, and Sister?

Read Luke 7:11–17 and John 19:25–28. Then answer the following questions:

1. What do these stories have in common?

2. What does Jesus do in each of them?

3. Why does Jesus do it?

4. What do these stories say about our responsibility to our parents and others' parents?

SCRIPTURE ACTIVITY

The Family of Moses

Read Exodus 2:1–10. Fill in what each of the characters do positively and negatively and how they obey or disobey the values protected by the fourth commandment.

CHARACTER	POSITIVE	NEGATIVE
A certain man of the house of Levi		
A Levite woman		
The sister		
The daughter of Pharaoh		

In light of this story, what are some of your responsibilities toward your brothers and sisters and other children?

___

___

___

GROUP ACTIVITY

The Future of the Family

The year is 2025. How old will you be? The mandatory retirement age is now fifty years old. Make a list of the things you *need* in order to live decently. (Assume that you are going to continue living for another thirty years.) Be sure to include all the basic necessities of life. How do you think they should be provided? What are you going to do in return for having received these necessities?

NECESSITIES	PROVIDED BY	WHAT YOU WILL DO IN RETURN

How old will your parents, grandparents, brothers, and sisters be in the year 2025? What do you think life will be like for you and for them?

_____

_____

_____

Draw a picture to illustrate what respect for the family will be like in the year 2025.

3 The Fifth Commandment:
Respect Life

PREPARATION PAGE

Fear and Violence

1. List the types of violence you have personally experienced.

2. List the types of violent acts that you yourself have committed.

3. What are you most afraid of having happen to you? Why does it make you so afraid?

READING ACTIVITY

The Dream of Becoming a Doctor

Sheila Cassidy had always wanted to be a doctor. So, in 1963, that's what she became. But her path had its ups and downs. She took many stiff examinations, lived on welfare to study, and worked sixty to eighty hours a week for six years in England's National Health Service. Sheila decided to specialize in surgery, and until 1971 she worked ten-hour days and was expected to work all night every third night, as well as all night and all day every third weekend. She began to wonder if this was really the way to live. Occasionally, she wondered if she had a vocation to religious life, but she could never really decide; instead, she would pass an exam and be thrown into school again, or she would fall in love and stop thinking about it.

In 1965, she met Consuelo, a young Chilean doctor studying in Oxford, and years later they shared an apartment. Through Consuelo, Sheila came to know about and be fascinated with Chile. In 1971, she decided to go abroad and leave the rat-race to work in a shanty-town clinic in Santiago, the capital city of Chile.

Alone in a foreign country, Sheila returned to practicing her faith. She made friends with the priests and sisters who worked with the poor in the downtown slums of the city. Soon she joined them in their attempts to provide food, shelter, and medical care, and to comfort the poor who faced unemployment and the loss of loved ones in a repressive military dictatorship. Then, in November 1975, she was arrested for having treated a wounded revolutionary.

Sheila Cassidy was interrogated and then tortured and put in solitary confinement for three weeks. She was transferred to a detention camp with one hundred other women for five weeks and she was then expelled from the country on December 29, 1975. The British ambassador was recalled from Chile in protest the next day. Since then, Sheila has testified for Amnesty International and other human rights groups about what she and others experienced in Chile, and she has written a book about her experiences entitled *The Audacity to Believe*.

In her preface to the book, Sheila explains why she writes and speaks in public:

> On the day that I left Chile, one of my fellow prisoners told me that since she had known me her opinion of Catholics had fallen even lower than it had been before. This hit me especially hard because I had secretly imagined myself to be living a life of splendid Christian witness among the Marxists. She said that when I decided not to speak about my prison experiences because of the risks involved she could hardly bring herself to speak to me. Her condemnation of me was for professing to be a

Christian without having the courage to act like one. It was then that I realized that I owed it to the members of the camp to speak out on their behalf.

The day she left, Bishop Jorge Hourton tried to see her off. He caught a glimpse of her and wrote in a column in the weekly church newspaper, *Comunidad Cristiana*:

> We went to see her off. . . . We only managed to catch a glimpse of her through the glass doors. Amongst many black forms she climbed the stairway of the enormous machine—a white figure outlined against the horizon of the distant city. From one cage to another, through any gap she found, she waved her long arm and smiled gaily in answer to the affectionate farewell of her friends. Now she was waving the same hand that had touched so many sick bodies in our Policlinica of the Northern Zone, where so many had known and loved her—an open, honest hand, incapable of deceit or violence, as we all well knew. Her final cage was a steel bird that swallowed her whole. As the majestic bird took off amongst the roar of the turbines, it seemed that it carried in its beak an immense olive branch.

Sheila Cassidy lives quietly and alone now in England, next door to a monastery, writing, praying, and living with the memories of what happened to her and what still happens to people everywhere in the world.

> I have the audacity to believe that people everywhere can have three meals a day for their bodies; education and culture for their minds and dignity, equality and freedom for their spirits. I believe that what self-centered men have torn down other-centered people can build up. I still believe that one day mankind will bow before the altars of God and be crowned triumphant over war and bloodshed, and nonviolent redemptive goodwill will proclaim the rule of the land. And the lion and the lamb shall lie down together and every man shall sit under his own vine and fig tree and none shall be afraid. I still believe that we shall overcome.

THINK IT OVER

1. What are the differences between the violence you have experienced in your life in the United States and the violence Sheila Cassidy experienced in England and then in Chile?
2. How do you usually deal with violence that is done to you, or that you see?
3. What do you think is the hardest thing about living with violence?

STUDY

Life Is Holy

The tradition of the commandments is intent on preserving life, especially in the face of persecution or hate. The Law and the prophets of the Old Testament are clear that Yahweh is the God of life and of all people. The fifth commandment is blunt: Thou shalt not murder—take life. And Jewish tradition goes even further. The Mishnah, a compendium of traditions and sayings, states: "One person alone was brought forth at the time of creation in order to teach us that one who destroys a single human soul is regarded as the destroyer of the whole world, while one who preserves a single human soul is regarded as the preserver of the whole world." And a contemporary Jewish rabbi named Abraham Joshua Heschel said, only a few months before he died, "Just to be is a blessing, just to live is holy." Our God wants us to live, and to remind us of that and to prove his love of life, he sent us his own life, Jesus, so that our lives would be rich beyond our wildest expectations. All the following commandments are based on the ones that went before: to worship God alone and to respect life.

The Seamless Garment of Life

Cardinal Joseph Bernardin of Chicago, in a talk that he gave in 1984, called Christians to adopt a consistent life ethic, "a seamless garment of life," as he termed it. His call is based on two points: the dimensions of the threats to life today and the value of our moral vision. He says:

> The range of application is all too evident; nuclear war threatens life on a previously unimaginable scale; abortion takes life daily on a horrendous scale; public executions are fast becoming weekly events in the most advanced technological society in history; and euthanasia is now openly discussed and even advocated. Each of these issues must be confronted as pieces of a larger pattern.

But he is also interested in positive moral responses to life, not just don'ts. Cardinal Bernardin goes on:

> The case for a consistent ethic of life—one which stands for the protection of the right to life and the promotion of the rights which enhance life from womb to tomb—manifests the positive potential of the Catholic moral and social tradition. It is both a complex and a demanding tradition; it joins the humanity of the unborn infant and the humanity of the hungry; it calls for positive legal action to prevent the killing of the unborn or the aged and positive societal action to provide shelter for the homeless and education for the illiterate . . . A consistent life ethic does not equate the problem of taking life (e.g., through abortion and in war) with the problem of promoting human

Just to be is a blessing, just to live is holy.

dignity (through humane programs of nutrition, health care, and housing). But a consistent life ethic identifies both the protection of life and its promotion as moral questions. It argues for a continuum of life which must be sustained in the face of diverse and distinct threats.

The "seamless garment" symbol refers to the garment Jesus wore at his crucifixion. Because it was only one piece of cloth and could not be split between people, it was not torn and the soldiers drew lots for it. It says that life—all life, anyone's life—is precious and that God holds human life in *his* hand. We, as children of God, are commanded: Thou shalt not kill.

Respect Life: No Abortion

What is abortion? In simple, physical or medical terms, it is based on the reality that 266 days following conception in a woman's body, another body emerges. The woman's body is a nurturing organism for another's life and possibility. The process and passage of life shared between human beings is inherently ordered, and it is the way all of us come into the world. Human development and physical development follow a continuum. Abortion is the choice to stop (abort) and to discontinue that growth of human life by violent interference. It is the physical choice to kill the unborn and the psychological choice to ignore and deny life, either by rationalizing away the fact of life and personhood or by ignoring the responsibility one has incurred in the creating of life by having sexual relations with another person.

There is an innate right to control one's body, both negatively and positively. We exercise that right by our choice of sleep, food, exercise, and daily use, as well as by how we satisfy our sexual and physical needs. Furthermore, we make choices that are medical: transplants, mastectomies, contraception and sterilization, the need for operations and radiation therapy—all of which involve our bodies and medical technology, affecting our lives and those of others. Some of these medical techniques entail protecting and continuing our own lives: transplants, operations, even radiation therapy that has many harmful side effects. We are even willing to lose pieces of our body in order to ensure that our lives will continue. Other medical choices entail curtailing life or its possibility: contraception and sterilization. But each of these choices is primarily focused on ourselves and our own concept of life.

It is here that the issue of control over one's body diverges in the question of abortion. No longer is the issue the quality of life of the woman, but the reality of life or no life for another. The focus has shifted. If we are willing to go to such lengths to ensure our own lives, then certainly, as Christians, we must go to the same lengths to ensure the life that is the result of our own behavior and personal choices. Pro-choice proponents say that a woman's life is more important than the unborn child's and that she alone can decide if the child's birth and presence will affect the style and quality of her own life. Physically, our sexuality and reproduction are intimately linked and designed to be looked at as a whole in making choices. Human happiness is important, but not at the expense of another's life or as the basis for moral choices.

Respect Life: Personal Violence

Whenever we think about violence, we have a tendency to assume that its cause and reality is founded only in other people, whether they are nations or groups or individuals who may be problematic for society. We think of the arms race or terrorists or criminals. In reality, however, the American people are part of what is sometimes referred to as a domestic arms race. There are approximately 120 million handguns in the United States, owned by private individuals. Almost half of all the homes in the country have them, some for sport and more for protection. But in a recent survey at the University of Tennessee, it was learned that the majority of those guns that were used in violent crimes were used on the owners themselves, their relatives, friends, or neighbors, and only a small portion on prowlers or intruders.

They studied 743 firearm-related deaths: 398 occurred in the home of the gun owner; 333 of these were suicides, fifty percent of the remaining sixty-five were homicides; twelve were accidental deaths; and three were of undetermined causes. Only two were used on intruders. Thus, the statistics indicate that gun owners took the lives of their friends or acquaintances twelve times more often than they stopped intruders and that they killed a member of their own household eighteen times more often than they killed a stranger. What does this say about our own fears, reactions, and tendencies toward violence?

What Is Life?

If this fifth commandment calls us to life and respect for life, then what is life? Usually, when someone asks what is the opposite of life, we say death. But that is not true. The opposite of death is birth, and life is what lies between those two momentous events. We are born, we live, and we die. Life encompasses all three of those realities. The dictionary has a number of definitions of life. One of them is "a human being," and another is "one's manner of being." We are *life,* and that life has been given to us and shared with us by God. It has been given to us for safekeeping and safeguarding. And we are to safeguard others, *all* others, as we safeguard our own. This is called the Golden Rule; but it is only a starting point for looking at and regarding life with respect and care. C.S. Lewis, in his book *Mere Christianity,* wrote:

> Do not waste time bothering whether you "love your neighbor"; act as if you did. As soon as we do this we will find one of the great secrets. When you are behaving as if you loved someone, you will presently come to love him. If you injure someone you dislike, you will find yourself disliking him more. If you do him a good turn, you will find yourself disliking him less.

We are life, and that life has been given to us and shared with us by God.

Joy

One of the qualities of life is joy, an attitude toward being human and alive that reflects a belief and delight in living. Respect for life is revealed in our own joy and ways of living. Jesus tells his disciples:

> Come to me, all you who labor and are burdened, and I will give you rest. Take my yoke upon you and learn from me, for I am meek and humble of heart; and you will find rest for yourselves. For my yoke is easy, and my burden light.
> Matthew 11:28–30

Joy is a gift and it is given to us when we share our lives with others. It's not like happiness, which is a feeling that can go as easily and quickly as it comes. Happiness is small in comparison with joy. Sheila Cassidy looked for happiness in a car, money, and reputation; when she went to Chile, she found joy in being with people who cared about others and about her. She cared for people as a doctor and as a human being. The women in jail with her were the very people who taught her joy and a deeper respect for life. Her vocation as a doctor was a choice for life and she honored it, by healing anyone who needed help. She was arrested and tortured because she honored her commitment to sustain life, everyone's life. Although her choice led to suffering, it also led to more life, despite fear and violence. The very choice of a title for her book—*The Audacity to Believe*—says much about courage and life: the audacity, the bravery, the intensity to believe—to believe in life, in goodness, in comfort and care, in respect for others. She stood on the side of life, even though that choice led to persecution.

We are called to stand on the side of life—to believe, encourage, support, affirm, and stand with those who hope and share life. And to begin is simple; it is to smile, to give compliments, to listen to others, to look around us and see what is going on in others' lives, and above all, to be grateful for what we have been given. The list of gifts and life that we already possess would be long: life itself, talents, sight, freedom of movement, education, wealth, options and dignity, a place in our families and society, our nation and all of its resources and possibilities, our faith, and our life in God by grace and the sacraments. These are just beginnings. Life is more than just enduring day to day; it has a quality of gracefulness and freedom and dignity that God has shared with us. We are free, free to imitate God's sharing of life, or we are free to destroy, tear down, belittle, or ignore the life around us and in us.

We are called to stand on the side of life.

WHAT ABOUT YOU?

1. When are you most aware of *not* being at peace?
2. What do you think is the connection between joy and life?
3. What are the similarities between capital punishment and abortion? (Use the seamless garment ethic in defense of all life to support your answer.)
4. Take a few of the experiences of violence that you have known. What does the seamless garment of life have to say to them?

SCRIPTURE ACTIVITY

The Violence Against Jesus' Life

Read the following Scripture passages. Describe how Jesus dealt with the violence he experienced in his own life.

SCRIPTURE	JESUS' RESPONSE
John 2:23–25	
John 5:16–18	
John 7:1–13	
John 11:45–54	
John 18:19–24	
Luke 22:39–46	

What are some positive responses to violence that Jesus practiced?

_____

_____

_____

SCRIPTURE ACTIVITY

Jesus' Response to Others' Violence

Look up these Scripture passages. How did Jesus respond to the violence other people committed?

SCRIPTURE	JESUS' RESPONSE
Mark 12:38–40	
Matthew 26:47–52	
Matthew 23:13–37	
Matthew 14:1–13	
Matthew 10:16–27	
Matthew 5:38–42	

GROUP ACTIVITY

Respecting Your Own Life

The fifth commandment, Thou shalt not kill, also refers to bad habits and destructive behavior that each of us can do to ourselves: drugs, drinking, promiscuous behavior, lack of sleep, sitting around doing nothing except watching TV, or any other kind of addictive behavior. Most often these activities are done with our friends or people we want to accept us and like us. What we do to ourselves and with others reveals either our respect for the life God has given to us or disrespect for life. List some of the things you think could be done to reflect how you feel about life (your own life and the lives of your friends). Think about whether or not you'd be willing to commit yourself to living up to the list.

WHAT YOU DO	HOW YOU FEEL	HOW TO RESPECT YOURSELF MORE

In the space below, write a code of conduct or an oath that you would be willing to follow that reveals your values toward life as a disciple of Jesus. You may want to model this oath on the Boy Scout or Girl Scout oaths.

I,_____,

4 The Sixth and Ninth Commandments:
Be Faithful and True

PREPARATION PAGE

How Do I Love Thee?

1. Who has loved you the longest?

2. Who has loved you the best?

3. What are the differences between these two kinds of love?

4. What is a friend for you? What is demanded between friends?

READING ACTIVITY

Poets and Friends

Osip Mandelstam was born in 1891, and by 1913 he was considered one of the best poets in Russia. By 1928, he was well known even outside of his own country, but his own personal position in the government was beginning to fall apart. His poetry was his way of responding to the political events of the Russian Revolution and the purges that followed in the 1920s and 1930s. "I cannot be silent," he said, and by 1933 a few brave people were beginning to talk about what Stalin was doing in Russia. There were mass deportations of peasants, writers were silenced; food and resources were rationed, and there was widespread murder and imprisonment.

Osip continued to write poetry, knowing that his words could get him in trouble. He once said, "Poetry is respected only in this country—people are killed for it. There's no place where more people are killed for it." He maintained that if they killed people for writing poetry, then they must also fear and respect it. Poetry, like fear and guns, had a power to bring people together. He called poetry "the yeast of the world, a sweet-voiced labor," and he believed he was only a poet when his mind was not deceitful and his work selfless: "a selfless song is its own praise, a comfort to friends, and pitch to enemies."

In 1934, Mandelstam was arrested for writing a poem that referred to Stalin and his grim work. Someone had informed on Mandelstam, and he was immediately jailed, interrogated, and kept apart from his wife and family. By some miracle he wasn't shot; instead, he was exiled to a small town in the Urals where he tried to kill himself. Later he and his wife were exiled to Voronezh.

Osip's wife kept him alive. Her name was Nadezhda, which in Russian means "hope." She was also an artist and a writer, and she spoke three or four languages besides Russian. She was with him in exile and literally kept him alive while they lived in fear. They returned to Moscow in 1937 only to find that they had lost their right to living space. They were homeless and unable to find work. They wandered for the next twelve months, living in terror. Osip had two heart attacks, and in May of 1938 they were again arrested. Osip was sentenced to five years of hard labor for "counter-revolutionary activities." He was put on a transport train in October 1938. His brother received notice that he had died on December 27, 1938.

But it is not only his poetry that is now remembered with awe in Russia; it is the marriage of Osip and Nadezhda Mandelstam, and their faithfulness to each other. They were married in 1919 and devoted their time together to writing. Then Osip decided to write that one poem as an act of defiance against the government. Their ordeal and their reliance on each other as husband and wife began. They lived in dire poverty in exile, shunned by everyone, in fear. And Nadezhda committed to memory every one of her husband's poems, all the rewrites and changes. She cared for him physically and stood by him in his sickness and his insanity that followed his time in prison. And in the years that followed his death (she didn't know until the late 1960s how and when he really died), she put all of his poetry—hundreds of poems—down on paper and wrote two books that portray their life together in the midst of the Stalin purges.

Osip Mandelstam was the poet, but Nadezhda was his hope, his wife, his friend and lover, and the woman who gave his poetry to the world by learning all of his words by heart and refusing to let him die in the memory of the Russian people. She died in her eighties, still writing of the love that gave meaning to both of their lives. Their friendship and faithfulness to their ideals and dreams, as well as their marriage, are remembered now around the world. She was buried as an Orthodox Christian.

THINK IT OVER

1. How was Nadezhda a friend to Osip?
2. What do you think held them together in the face of what they had to endure?
3. What does marriage and faithfulness mean to you?

STUDY
Laws and Loves

It all begins in a garden: Eden. In Genesis 1 and 2, God creates man and woman in his image, telling them to multiply and subdue the earth and that it is not good for man to be alone. Here in the garden, sexuality and marriage are bound together, as companionship and generation, as friendship and faithfulness to each other.

Marriage is a social institution, an economic arrangement, and society's structure for perpetuating the race. It can also be a human relationship that is born of friendship and love. Marrying for love is a relatively new phenomenon. In the Old Testament, the only person married for love is Rachel—and Jacob works fourteen years for her, receiving Leah after the first seven years of work. In Jewish society, marriage held the nation together.

Divorce was allowed, but primarily for men. Moses changed the law because of the hardness of his people's hearts. The law in Jewish society discriminated against women. The woman caught in adultery was to be stoned to death, while the man got off with a warning. This is the law that Jesus questions in Matthew's Gospel (19:3–9). In Luke's account, the comments on divorce and marriage are given as ethical directives, not laws. But what Jesus does say is worth noticing: "Everyone who divorces his wife and marries another commits adultery, and the one who marries a woman divorced from her husband commits adultery" (16:18). Jesus says that the Jewish law is not correct. He says that marriage unites a man and woman in such a way that the law cannot dissolve it. And he says that the obligations are not only on the part of the woman, but also on the man's. Jesus sees man and woman as equal partners with equal rights.

Jesus and Marriage

Jesus does not lay down laws. He always frames his commandments and his calls to a change of life within the context of relationships, especially our relationship to God who lays direct claim to us. The law can never really protect a marriage; that is done by the two who are married, the community to which they belong, and God, who is a part of the marriage. God's words are a demand and a promise. His words talk about the heart of the matter, not just the law. Marriages fail, but to concentrate on the failures is to do a disservice to those who love. Jesus quotes Genesis on the meaning of marriage:

> Have you not read that from the beginning the Creator "made them male and female" and said, "For this reason a man shall leave his father and mother and be joined to his wife, and the two shall become one flesh"? So they are no longer two, but one flesh. Therefore, what God has joined together, no human being must separate.
>
> Matthew 19:4–6

God is the witness to marriage, to the relationship. What the relationship of love is, who the two are together in the marriage, is important. The relationship becomes a sacrament, a mystery that is called to image God's faithfulness to us, his undying love for us, his forgiveness and mercy, his steadfastness, and his friendship.

Marriage for Christians

Marriage for Christians is a choice for life with friendship and faithfulness. Two people choose to take care of each other's souls and to try to live together in an absorbing mystery of two persons who are communion for each other. It is an art that takes time, experience, mistakes, and confusion. It is a discipline of friendship and faithfulness given as a gift to one other person.

It is in light of this enduring friendship that the commandments of no adultery, no extramarital sex, no premarital sex, no divorce, and the question of birth control must be seen.

These specific failures to live up to the marriage are an effect of the breakdown of friendship and enduring love. The positive aspects of discipline and shared love make a marriage: kindness, unselfishness, truth, integrity, privacy, right use of sexuality, other friends, prayer, worship, and the sacraments. Any betrayal of the marriage happens long before specific commandments are disobeyed. There is an old Chinese saying: "I am interested in what remains after a pot is broken." Failure in relationship is human, but as Christians we are called to forgive, to reconcile, to begin again, and to rely on God for our strength. Marriages are like journeys: arriving is not as important as how one travels there.

If such a friendship of body, soul, heart, mind, and spirit existed and broke apart, then such failure needs to be repented and lives changed so that the causes do not continue to tear others apart. In these commandments we are called to faithfulness, to be the friends of God to those we choose to marry in the Lord.

Friendship and Faithfulness

Each of us has standards of what we look for and come to expect in a friend. Friendship is the basis of love in marriage, and it is what faithfulness is built on within the context and grace of the sacrament of Marriage. Marriage for Christians is not the same as marriage in a civil court. It demands and gives much more.

The nature of marriage, the tying together of friendship and faithfulness, makes it a relationship of endurance, unlike any other relationship. The Preparation Page questions in this chapter asked who has loved you the longest and who has loved you the best. Usually our parents or one of them has loved us the longest. Time or endurance is a quality of love and friendship. But the person who loves us best teaches us and introduces us to another kind of love, the intensity and depth of love that comes from marriage, the bonding in sexuality and children through faithfulness. It is a relationship that is worked at, created by two people together with God.

Marriage for Christians is a choice for life with friendship and faithfulness.

Marriage and Community

Marriage for Christians is a sacrament that binds two people together in the presence of the community that believes with them that marriage is an image of the presence and love of God with his people. The religious symbolism of marriage is that of the Trinity: two persons who freely and publicly acknowledge their love for each other and call on God to witness their love and to be a part of it, the source of it. This promise is celebrated in the community, both as support for their relationship and as a living, breathing example of love. Two Christians say that they will be faithful to each other as God is faithful to his people. It is a covenant based on love and on faith in God which is meant to grow stronger and truer with time and intensity. The community bears witness and affirms the love between the couple and God. It is a life-giving relationship that calls out unselfishness, kindness, creativity, warmth and affection, trust, hospitality, and freedom to love others more and more.

The characteristics of a good marriage and friendship that is faithful are the characteristics of God in relation to us: forgiveness, understanding, truth-telling, encouragement, mercy, compassion, and integrity. The breaking of the sixth or ninth commandments puts in jeopardy the very core of the relationship of love.

Extramarital Sexuality

The bonding of two people in marriage is built on trust and vulnerability, sharing their bodies, souls, and hearts with each other. Genital sexuality is only understood and experienced honestly and religiously within the context of marriage, of public faithfulness. Not to harm the other includes not lying and not sharing with another what has been promised and given to one's lover and marriage partner. It is responsible love—love that carries the other in one's heart and that takes care that the other is first in any decision making.

Sexual bonding through genital sexuality encompasses the emotions, bodies, hearts, and souls of the two people. It draws them outside of themselves and gives them to each other in trust. That mutual trust is creative and life-giving, both to the two who are married and also to children. Children are the natural possibility and outcome of consistently shared love between two people. To break that bond by engaging in genital sexuality with another, whether married or single, is to tear that relationship violently. But the act itself is not the only failure. The failure also comes in the dishonesty, the exclusion of the other partner, and the breakdown in integrity and the breaking of the promise to love and cherish and tend to the other partner's welfare.

Limits on the Relationship

Marriage for those who believe in God and in Jesus Christ is a relationship that has no limits. We are called to grow into love that reflects the love of God in our lives, and there is no limit to that

> *We are called to be the friends of God to those we choose to marry in the Lord.*

love. It is expansive, outgoing, diffusive, and extravagant. It is the handing over of our lives, bodies, and souls in trust to another. It is saying that we will love that person as God has loved us and that we want everyone to watch and see how God dwells among us today.

But all of us have ways of putting limits and boundaries on a relationship. It can mean slowly not being honest, choosing not to speak, listen, or care about the other. Or it can go deeper, collecting hurts and pains and then refusing to forgive or to become vulnerable again. Or it can develop into the decision to take care of one's own needs first, either emotionally or physically, by going to someone else. The act of adultery is the end of a long series of choices to limit love and the giving of oneself.

Birth Control as a Limit to Love

But there are other ways, within a marriage, to limit love and not to trust either the other person or God. One of those ways is to decide not to have children or to limit the possibility of children. Marriage is not simply a legal arrangement for taking care of one's sexual needs or a license to sleep with another. It is a commitment to mirror what it means to be human and graced: to love and let that love extend beyond us into our children, the visible sign of having love and loving each other. To decide that children are a problem or an unwanted effect of love is to bring into serious doubt the quality and depth of the love between two people. There are two reasons for being married: to build up and nurture the bond of friendship and love between man and woman, and to bring forth children that keep that love alive, honest, and whole.

God is an integral factor in every Christian marriage, and to decide lightly or arbitrarily (without consulting a priest or counselor) not to have children is to betray a lack of trust in God. There is the responsibility not only to have children but to nurture them and care for them to the best of one's ability. Love draws us beyond ourselves and calls us to make room for another or others.

The Expressions of Love

There are no boundaries to the expressions of love, only imagination, creativity, and grace. The obvious expressions of touch, physical closeness, companionship, and sexual pleasure are meant to build on and extend to emotional and psychological closeness and intimacy. Shared secrets, small details, compliments, terms of endearment, shared suffering and discouragement, mutual friends, and especially times apart are all examples of expressions of love. But there are other important expressions of love between two people who are lovers in God. Prayer, the sacraments, liturgy, solitude, and retreat time together, even the discipline of shared abstinence, call each person in the marriage to concretely put the other's welfare of body and soul first.

Marriages endure, and couples promise to be faithful, despite hardship, suffering, sickness, disappointments, unfaithfulness, and dishonesty. "Until death do us part" does not mean "until we feel like it or it gets rough or I want something more." There is the demand to work out issues and problems together. And for that, each partner needs prayer and a strong relationship with God, as well as prayer for and with each other and friends that support their values, life-styles, and the Christian belief in the faithfulness of love.

The Effect on Society of Marriage and Divorce

The choice of two individuals to marry is not limited to that couple alone. Marriage is part of society's structure to maintain stability and to bind generations together. The economic and sociological structure of nations is based on marriage and family. A marriage that fails affects children, parents, grandparents, friends, and everyone who knows the couple, especially on a religious level. To fail is understandable and forgivable, but it must also be dealt with honestly.

It is often said that there is a problem with divorce in the United States, even within the Catholic Church. But there is more of a problem with marriage. Marriage needs to be prepared for and entered into with as much preparation as any vocation or choice of job or profession. That is why the Church demands and asks couples who are planning to marry to study, to attend seminars, and to share their ideals, values, goals, and doubts beforehand. The wedding ceremony is not magic; it is only a beginning, a hope proclaimed. The marriage is made throughout a lifetime of trial, error, forgiveness, trying again, reconciliation, prayer, and support from others, as well as times of going it alone and struggling through difficult times together. The Church is there to support and teach and help. The Church in this case is the institution that calls the couple beyond themselves with grace, as well as ordinary people who are married and single, trying together with others to live up to their baptismal and marriage commitments so that others can see how believers in Jesus struggle to be consistent about loving and being faithful to one another.

Homosexuality

The reality of genital sexuality is always seen in the context of faithfulness and public commitment to another in marriage. Marriage calls the couple to extend and deepen their own love and to bring forth others through their expression of love. Creation and love are bound together. It is in light of this call to faithfulness and responsibility in terms of sexuality that homosexuality is seen as a failure of obedience to these commandments.

Homosexuality needs to be defined. It is the inclination towards one's own gender and the practice of genital sexuality in that context. One can commit homosexual acts without being a homosexual. Homosexuality is the term usually applied to male sexual practice, and lesbianism is the term used for female sexual practice and/or inclination.

Each person is a sexual being, and each person has wants, needs, and desires that demand attention. But Christians believe that, as human beings, we are called to express our sexuality and respond to those physical needs in the context of a relationship that is faithful, public, and loving. Any act or relationship based on selfishness, primary care of oneself, pleasure, or ego is destructive of others, whether within a marriage or outside of it. All people are called to integrity, to purity, and to primary trust in God as the one who loves us, cares for us, and created us in his image to love others. This way of living as a Christian is learned—just as anything is learned—with others, through mistakes, forgiveness, reconciliation, and rededication to our values, which are the values of God.

WHAT ABOUT YOU?

1. What do you think is the worst thing you could do in a marriage besides the act of committing adultery? Why?
2. What is the worst thing you can do in any friendship? Would that break up the relationship for you?
3. If God *always* forgives us, what does that say about our relationships? How faithful do we have to be?
4. Do you agree that marriage is a lifetime commitment, with God as a witness? How does that make you feel?
5. What is the relationship of children to husband and wife? What qualities of friendship make it natural to have children in a marriage?

SCRIPTURE ACTIVITY

Friends and Faithfulness

Read the following Scripture passages and describe the qualities of friendship and faithfulness that are mentioned.

SCRIPTURE	QUALITIES
Ruth 1:16–17a	
1 Samuel 18:1, 3	
John 15: 9–17	
Luke 22:60	
Matthew 26: 47–50	

SCRIPTURE ACTIVITY

Jesus' Values on Marriage and Faithfulness

Study the following Scripture passages in which Jesus has some specific things to say about marriage, adultery, or divorce. For each of the passages, write down Jesus' values on marriage and sexuality.

John 8:1–11

John 4:1–18

Matthew 19:3–9

GROUP ACTIVITY

Betrayal and Sin

I. Do this exercise individually. Then, as a group, try to come to a consensus on what is wrong and why. Rank in order of what you think is the worst thing you can do, with reasons:

_____ Premarital sex
Reason for ranking: _____

_____ Extramarital sex
Reason for ranking: _____

_____ Betraying a confidence
Reason for ranking: _____

_____ Betraying a friend in public
Reason for ranking: _____

_____ Divorce
Reason for ranking: _____

_____ Birth control
Reason for ranking: _____

_____ Trial marriage
Reason for ranking: _____

_____ Not to forgive adultery
Reason for ranking: _____

_____ Lying and betraying confidences in a marriage
Reason for ranking: _____

II. Choose the top three actions from the previous page. As a group, discuss the choices and come to a consensus concerning the worst failures against the sixth and ninth commandments.

1. _____

2. _____

3. _____

III. What actions and attitudes constitute unfaithfulness for you? Why?

IV. As a group, what is the basis of unfaithfulness?

5 The Seventh and Tenth Commandments:
Live Simply

PREPARATION PAGE

If I Were A Rich Man!

1. If you had $100,000, what would you do with it?

2. What do you think it means when someone says you're "poor"?

3. What do you own right now?

READING ACTIVITY

Francis the Poor Man

High in the ceiling of the Lower Basilica of St. Francis in Assisi, there is a fresco depicting a wedding ceremony attended by angels. It is Christ who gives the bride to a young monk, Francis. The bride is Lady Poverty. They are standing on a rock and Francis is putting a ring on her finger.

Lady Poverty is gaunt, pale, dressed in rags, and beautiful. Two street urchins are taunting her, one getting ready to throw a rock and the other threatening her with a stick. Behind her is a rosebush in bloom, and at her feet is a pile of thorns. The fresco was painted by Giotto, and it tries to describe Francis' attitude toward possessions, security, and money.

Francis came from an affluent family. His father was a cloth merchant, and Francis most probably grew up learning the business. He was known to dress in the latest fashions and to spend the profits of his father's business on parties and on his friends.

Money had gained status in the twelfth century, and bartering was going out of style. Goods and possessions took up space and had to be stored and preserved; money, however, could be hoarded, loaned, and accumulated much more easily. The growth of cities had a strong effect on the economy and greed was prevalent, as was the gap between the rich and the poor. Poverty, deformity, illness, and leprosy were intertwined barriers to relationships and community.

When Francis was converted and turned to Jesus, he opened the Scriptures three times. These are the passages he found: "If you wish to be perfect, go, sell what you have and give to the poor.... Then come, follow me" (Matthew 19:21); "Take nothing for the journey, neither walking stick, nor sack, nor food, nor money" (Luke 9:3); "Whoever wishes to come after me must deny himself, take up his cross, and follow me" (Matthew 16:24). Francis loved poverty and called it "his Lady."

For Francis, possessiveness was the root cause of many of the world's evils: violence, war, greed, selfishness. And so he set out to dispossess himself of goods. He lived like the poor, helping them with alms and work because of his compassion for them. He wanted his brothers to dress like the poor and nothing was to be considered theirs. They were to live as pilgrims and strangers in the world. They were to work, like the poor, and if they did not receive a just salary for their work, they were not to say anything, but instead beg for what they needed. They were never to receive money; only in necessity could they receive alms like other poor people.

The brothers were not to cling to learning, wisdom, natural talents, or even their virtues. They were to belong only to God and they were to see everything, even their lives, as entrusted to them by him. They were not to claim any power or prestige or great skill—even in preaching—but they were to be humble of heart, like Jesus.

Francis prayed, "O holy Lady Poverty, may the Lord keep you with your sister holy Humility."

This kind of humility and poverty was expressed in love, and out of this kind of living came Francis's joy, passion, delight in the world, freedom, dignity, and laughter. He was a troubadour and minstrel, preaching to the birds, converting and taming wolves, courteous to fire, and mad with devotion to God. He wanted to be like his Master, and he often quoted: "Foxes have dens and birds of the sky have nests, but the Son of Man has nowhere to rest his head" (Matthew 8:20). He couldn't live better than his master had lived. The people he loved most and best were the poor—especially those who were poorer than himself and the poor Christ. There are stories that even the only copy of the New Testament that the brothers used in prayer was given to a poor woman to sell for what she needed because they believed that the giving of alms was more important than reading about poverty and goodness.

Francis made friends with animals, but more so with birds. Birds have often been associated with angels and messages from God, and Francis called them his sisters. Legends say the swallows would twitter noisily whenever he would come to preach in the piazza in Orvieto, and they would become quiet so that he could preach. A black raven kept him company during his final retreat on Mount Alverna.

When it came time for Francis to die, he was blind, sick, and in terrible pain. He asked his brothers to carry him back to the Porziuncula (where he had first promised his life to Lady Poverty) and to place him on the ground, naked. He told them to leave him there after he died for as long as "it takes a man to walk a mile leisurely." He died as he had promised he would live—with nothing but his love and his freedom.

THINK IT OVER

1. What do you find most attractive about Saint Francis?
2. Would it be difficult to live as Saint Francis did? Why or why not?
3. How do you think people would react to him if he lived today?
4. How would you react to him?

STUDY

What Must I Do to Have Eternal Life?

In Mark's gospel there is a story that has much to say about possessions, following Jesus, and obeying his commandment, his invitations. It is the story of the rich young man.

> As he was setting out on a journey a man ran up, knelt down before him, and asked him, "Good teacher, what must I do to inherit eternal life?" Jesus answered him, "Why do you call me good? No one is good but God alone. You know the commandments: 'You shall not kill; you shall not commit adultery, you shall not steal; you shall not bear false witness; you shall not defraud; honor your father and your mother.'" He replied and said to him, "Teacher, all of these I have observed from my youth." Jesus, looking at him, loved him and said to him, "You are lacking in one thing. Go, sell what you have, and give it to the poor and you will have treasure in heaven; then come, follow me." At that statement his face fell, and he went away sad, for he had many possessions.
>
> Mark 10:17–27

We don't know if the young man ever came back. The story just ends there. What he owned, what he had, got in the way of following Jesus. He had tried all of his life to be obedient, and he now wanted to be closer to Jesus. The Scripture says that Jesus looked at him with love as the young man told him what he wanted. Still, he couldn't respond to Jesus' words. His possessions meant more to him than Jesus.

This is what the seventh and the tenth commandments are concerned with: being more attached to what we own or what we want (covet) than being concerned about obeying God and drawing closer to him. To steal—the action of taking from another what is theirs and not ours—and to covet—to desire and want something someone else has so much that we can't think of anything else—are warnings. We are owned by anything that has that kind of control over us, but we are only to be owned by God.

The story goes on, and it is our story too:

> Jesus looked around and said to his disciples, "How hard it is for those who have wealth to enter the kingdom of God!" The disciples were amazed at his words. So Jesus again said to them in reply, "Children, how hard it is to enter the kingdom of God! It is easier for a camel to pass through the eye of a needle than for one who is rich to enter the kingdom of God." They were exceedingly astonished and said among themselves, "Then who can be saved?" Jesus looked at them and said, "For human beings it is impossible, but not for God. All things are possible for God."
>
> Mark 10:23–28

The seventh and the tenth commandments tell us what *not* to do—don't steal and don't covet, don't want what you don't need. But, to be a Christian, this means to share what you don't need, to be appreciative of what you do have, not to hold onto it too tightly because God is sharing it with you for now. We are to be stewards, or caretakers, of our possessions, our talents, our property, our money, our intellects, and our opportunities. We are not to be squirrels, hoarding and storing up while others are in need. And, certainly, we are not to steal or covet and betray the words of our prayer: "Give us this day our daily bread." For as children of God, brothers and sisters of Jesus, we say we trust that God will take care of us, that he knows what we need even before we ask, and that he is gracious and caring of us as a father takes care of his children.

Like all the others, the seventh and the tenth commandments remind us that God is the only God we are to follow and obey, and when possessions become more important than obeying God, then we are breaking his law. What we covet and steal is an idol that we worship more than God.

The Rule of Poverty

Francis and his brothers and sisters owned no property or possessions and roamed the earth, begging their way, living with the poor and working with them for meals. They repaired and rebuilt small chapels, and in winter, the cold forced them to build hedges, walls, and cells to keep the wind out. Francis was called *Il Poverello,* "the little poor man," poor in body and in spirit. He relied in faith on the first Beatitude: Blessed are the poor in spirit for the kingdom of heaven *is* theirs. The first and last Beatitudes are written in the present tense. He and his brothers indeed tried to make present the joy, simplicity, and truthfulness of the kingdom of God for their neighbors in Assisi and the surrounding towns.

Francis' poverty was a way of acting, a way of choosing, rather than *not* choosing. It was a choice to imitate Christ, to walk with the poor who have no choice, to be humble as Jesus was humble in coming down to us from heaven, to live close to the earth, praising Brother Sun, Sister Moon, Mother Earth, Father Sky, and God for his blessings on us through all of creation. Francis's poverty was paradoxical, like much of Jesus' teachings in the Gospel: To lose everything and save your soul, to lose your life and to gain everlasting life in resurrection, strength in weakness, light in darkness, fullness by being emptied out and given over to God.

An early Franciscan poet, Jacopone da Todi, sings of this positive sense of poverty and the freedom it brings in a poem:

> The earth and all the plants that grow;
> The trees, and all the fruits they show,
> The very beasts, my yoke that know—
> All in my homestead I unite.
> The running waters, lake and sea,
> And all the fishes swimming free.
> The birds in windy air that be,

When possessions become more important than obeying God, then we are breaking his law.

These are the stuff of my delight.
Since to God's will my being clings,
I am the possessor of all things;
So many feathers have my wings,
To heaven it is an easy flight.

Poverty in Today's World

In today's society, Francis and his devotion to Lady Poverty has often been romanticized. The movie *Brother Sun, Sister Moon* was lyrically beautiful, but it did not do justice to the discipline of poverty that Francis and his friends practiced. In the Middle Ages, poverty was grinding, and the majority of people only knew hunger and deprivation. Poverty hasn't changed much in the eight hundred years since the time of Francis. The majority of the world still only knows hunger, want, frustration, and hardship in the face of plenty.

There are a few definitions of poverty that help us to see more clearly what the virtue of poverty might be. Physical poverty is the lack of the basic necessities of life: food, clothing, shelter, medicine, education, human dignity, and freedom. It is a way of living where life is daily jeopardy and survival is from day to day or from meal to meal. Another way of looking at poverty is to realize that people are poor when, every time they make a choice, it has life-threatening consequences. For example, those who have no health insurance must take their children to the hospital, and to pay for those medical expenses means that the rest of the family will not eat for the rest of the week. So poverty, in this case, is having no option or freedom in dealing with life situations.

And then there is the *virtue* of poverty, as opposed to the reality and fact of poverty. The virtue of poverty is the free choice to give up what one has so that others can have what they need to live, or to share with others their burden of life, in witness to the love of God sharing his life with us. In a practical sense, it can mean fasting from food and giving the money to those who need it. It can mean sharing possessions and home with those who need our extras in order to survive with some dignity. Or, it can mean working in a soup kitchen or collecting clothes or working on legislation that helps people live with dignity.

Like Francis and Jesus, the virtue of poverty is more a choice to be with, to share with, and to do without, than it is a burden. It connects us with people in love and care and comfort, and it says to those who lack basic necessities, love, support, or hope that we care, we care enough to give of some of our own possessions. Francis, like Jesus, lived a radical surrender to this virtue, but the virtue of poverty has many levels of meaning and understanding.

The Widow's Mite

Jesus publicly praises only a few people in the Gospel stories: John the Baptist; Mary, who washes his feet before his death; and the widow who gives a mite—a penny, nothing much to those who are watching.

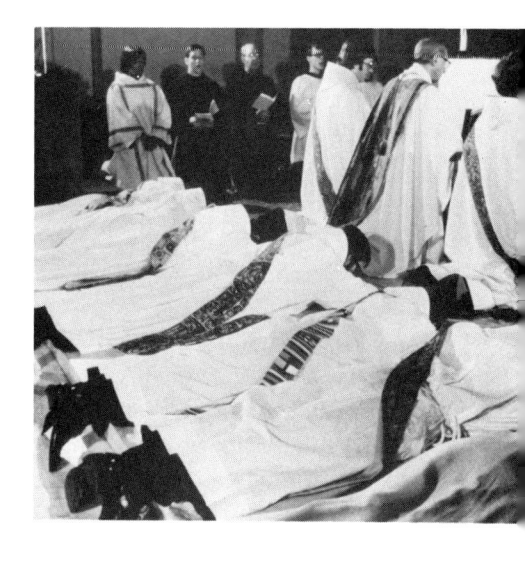

> *The virtue of poverty is more a choice to be with, to share with, and to do without, than it is a burden.*

> [Jesus] sat down opposite the treasury and observed how the crowd put money into the treasury. Many rich people put in large sums. A poor widow also came and put in two small coins worth a few cents. Calling his disciples to himself, he said to them, "Amen, I say to you, this poor widow put in more than all the other contributors to the treasury. For they have all contributed from their surplus wealth, but she, from her poverty, has contributed all she had, her whole livelihood."
>
> Mark 12:41–44

The virtue of poverty lies in the free gift that we share with others, and we *know* in our bodies and souls that it is given not just from our extra but that it is something of ours that leaves a hole, either financially or emotionally. The virtue of poverty is closely tied to trusting in God and in others to be generous and to share what they have with those in need. We learn to practice this virtue like any other: by doing it both when it's easy and when it's not so easy. But the reason for doing it is always the same: others' need or love of God and wanting to share with others some of the gratitude for what God has given us and done for us. And so, the more we are grateful and the more we love, the more we give and share with others.

The Virtue of Thankfulness

Just as the opposite of not stealing is giving and sharing, the opposite of coveting is being thankful, of being grateful to God. Coveting is always wanting more and being greedy, while gratitude reminds us of God's graciousness to us and that all we have—our lives and possessions—are gifts from God. We are not to become squirrels, hiding and storing up everything we own, but we are to share what we have with others. We must live a life that shows that we are God's and that he takes care of us. We are more valuable to him than all else in his creation. To be mindful of God and his daily, minute-by-minute care for us is to sense joy and freedom, just as Francis did. He sang because he was free and because God shared everything with him. C.S. Lewis said, "Relying on God has to begin all over again every day, as if nothing had yet been done." And if we are thankful, then one of the practices we learn to do almost naturally is to welcome others into our lives, our families, our parishes, and our churches. There is always enough to go around when it is shared in the presence of God.

Hospitality

There are many ancient traditions that have to do with hospitality, of welcoming the stranger or anyone in need. In the Book of Genesis, Abraham welcomes three strangers, or angels, into his tent and kills his fatted calf for them, prepares a lavish meal, and honors them with food and drink. The Jewish people believed that God often visited his people under the guise of a stranger. It was required that any visitor be treated honorably as a guest for three days and given food, water, and rest. The first day was to recover from the journey or whatever had gone before. The second was to eat and share friendship and conversation with those who welcomed him. And the third day was to help the guest prepare to leave again and travel.

Later, when the Passover Supper became the central ritual of the Jewish nation, and after the death of the prophet Elijah, there was and still is the tradition that an empty place is set at the supper table and the door is left open, so that any passing stranger or person in need may come in and be welcomed as a friend at the table. The tradition is that God roams the world as a beggar and a stranger to see if he is welcomed or turned out. When he is accepted and treated with care, then the world is ready for the Messiah.

In the Christian tradition, this virtue of hospitality is almost the core of the Christian message: We are to treat and welcome everyone as Christ among us.

The Spiritual and Corporal Works of Mercy

How we treat the stranger, the hungry, and the sick, the lonely, and the imprisoned is how God will treat us (Matthew 25). The practical actions are traditionally known as the spiritual and corporal works of mercy.

One person who today illustrates Francis' love of poverty and the life-style it evokes is Mother Teresa of Calcutta. She says: "I try to give to the poor people for love what the rich could get for money. No I wouldn't touch a leper for a thousand pounds sterling, yet I willingly cure him for the love of God." Whenever Mother Teresa talks about the poor, she reminds people that they are really "Christ in the distressing disguise of the poor." Mother Teresa, like Francis, seems radical in how she lives, but at one time she was like anyone else. She learned by doing, by practicing and changing her own attitudes and behavior. We begin by sharing with others what we don't need, and as we share more, then we find it easier.

There is a sign in many Catholic Worker soup kitchens and houses of hospitality. It reads, "Thank more, need less" and often penciled in or scratched with magic marker are the words, "Thank more, eat less." But a way of choosing, a way of living that imitates Mother Teresa, Francis, and of course, Jesus himself begins simply: by sharing what you have with someone who needs it. William Penn, the founder of the Quakers, put it simply: "If there is any kindness I can show, or any good thing I can do to any fellow being, let me do it now, and not deter or neglect it, as I shall not pass this way again." Our God is a God of poverty: he gave up everything to be one of us, to share his life of grace with us. The positive response to these commandments calls us to imitate God, relying on the Father and trusting in Jesus and his community, the Church, for what we need, when we share with one another.

To steal, to covet, to take what isn't ours is to settle for too little. We are offered the kingdom of God now, when we share what we have and who we are with the poor and with all who are in need.

We are offered the kingdom of God now, when we share what we have and who we are with the poor and with all who are in need.

WHAT ABOUT YOU?

1. When you want something, how do you usually go about getting it?
2. Have you ever had anything stolen from you? How did you feel?
3. Have you ever thought that you are stealing from God when you do not use possessions and money rightly?
4. What do you think is the difference between sharing and poverty?

SCRIPTURE ACTIVITY

Jesus' Ideas about Money

Look up the following Scripture passages. Based on your reading, how are we to use rightly what has been given to us by God?

SCRIPTURE	RIGHT USE
Luke 16:9–12	
Luke 21:1–4	
Luke 20:20–26	

SCRIPTURE ACTIVITY

The Right Use of Gifts

Look up the following Scripture passages. How are we to use rightly what has been given to us by God?

SCRIPTURE	RIGHT USE
Luke 19:8–10	
Luke 19:11–27	
Luke 14:33–35	
Luke 16:1–8	
Luke 12:32–34	

The Seventh and Tenth Commandments: Live Simply   77

GROUP ACTIVITY

Possessions

In the space below, list or draw *your* possessions or anything to which you are attached. Then trade books with someone sitting near you. Look at their barn. Is there anything in their barn that you want? What can you do to get it? Make some sort of deal with the person who owns it. Return the book and, in your own barn, make any necessary changes to what you now own.

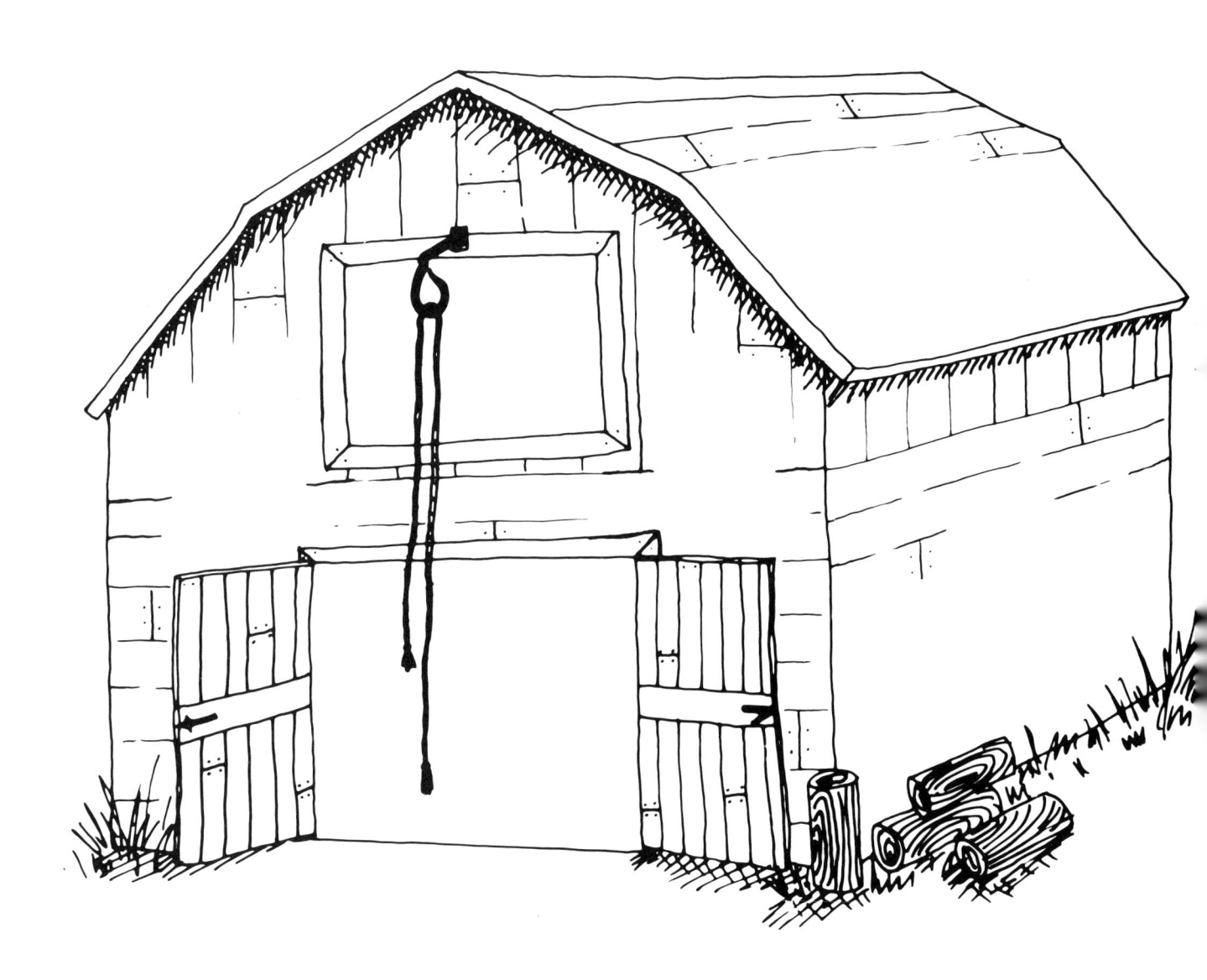

Stealing

1. What would you ever be willing to steal? Why?

2. What do you think are the causes of stealing?

3. What is restitution?

4. *Situation:* A classmate is caught stealing the answers to a test. What would be a fair punishment or restitution?

5. *Situation:* A corporation is convicted of bilking its customers out of a great deal of money. What would be a fair punishment or restitution?

6 The Eighth Commandment:
Be Truthful

PREPARATION PAGE

On Your Honor

1. When you try to lie, are you aware of anything that happens to you, physically or psychologically?

2. Have you ever gotten into trouble for telling the truth? How did you feel afterward?

3. If you had information that would change another person's opinion of someone (either positively or negatively), how would you use that information?

READING ACTIVITY

A Woman Known by Her Words

May 1942 It is sometimes hard to take in and comprehend, oh God, what those created in Your likeness do to each other in these disjointed days. But I no longer shut myself away in my room, God, I try to look things straight in the face, even the worst crimes, and to discover the small, naked human being amidst the monstrous wreckage caused by man's senseless deeds. . . . I try to face up to Your world, God, not to escape from reality into beautiful dreams—though I believe that beautiful dreams can exist beside the most horrible reality—and I continue to praise Your creation, God, despite everything.

Her name was Etty Hillesum. She was twenty-eight years old, a Jewish student living and studying in Holland and caught in the Nazi push to move all the Jews out of Holland and into the concentration camps and the gas chambers in Poland. She was a translator, a poet, and a writer. The Jews were confined to house arrest, wore yellow armbands, and were only permitted in certain areas of the city, only allowed to buy food at certain times. As the months wore on, communications between family and friends became more and more of a challenge of clandestine meetings, stolen paper and stamps, and non-Jewish friends carrying letters and packages.

Etty kept a diary of her prayers and questions. She began to look at death. She accepted destruction as a part of life, and she no longer wasted energies on the fear of dying. She faced it.

By July of 1943, members of her family were being "selected" for the boxcars and sent to Poland. She was "selected" for Westerbork, a camp on the border of Holland and Poland, the last stopping place for the death trains. Her job was to prepare people to leave—to leave Holland and to leave life. She knew what was on the other side of the border, though she never mentioned it. She gathered clothing, food, a spoon and bowl; she comforted mothers and children, cared for the sick, and wrote letters, postcards, and her journal, smuggling them out of the camp through friends.

> One thing is becoming increasingly clear to me: that You cannot help us, that we must help You to help ourselves. And that is all we can manage these days and also all that really matters; that we safeguard that little piece of You, God, in ourselves. And perhaps in others as well . . . . You cannot help us but we must help You and defend Your dwelling place inside us to the last. . . . No one is in their clutches who is in Your arms.

Etty lived in a desperate time, in desperate circumstances, with the German army closing in on all of western Europe. She was one person, one woman, and she continued to care for people knowing she was giving them small kindnesses before a crowded ride in a boxcar and a gas chamber at the end of the tracks. Yet, she still could see something of mystery and grace in what was happening around her.

The last entry in her journal is dated 12/10/42. "A soul is forged out of fire and rock crystal. Something rigorous, hard in an Old Testament sense, but also as gentle as the gesture with which his tender fingertips sometimes stroked my eyelashes." She knew she was leaving for the Westerbork camp in the morning. "Today will be a hard day. . . . When I suffer for the vulnerable is it not for my own vulnerability that I really suffer? I have broken my body like bread and shared it out among men. And why not, they were hungry and had gone without for so long. . . . We should be willing to act as a balm for all wounds." That is the end of the her diary.

On September 7, 1943, Etty Hillesum was deported to Auschwitz without warning. Her father, mother, and brother Mischa were in a freight car behind her. She had been a camp inmate for two months. She wrote in a letter to a friend: "I see more and more that love for all our neighbors, for everyone made in God's image, must take pride of place over love for one's nearest and dearest." On the way to her death, she threw a postcard out of the boxcar. Some farmers picked it up and mailed it back to her friends. It said: "Opening the Bible at random I find this: 'The Lord is my high tower.' . . . We left the camp singing. . . ." The records state the Etty Hillesum died in Auschwitz on November 30, 1943.

THINK IT OVER

1. How do you think you'd react in circumstances such as Etty's?
2. What do you think is the worst evil facing the world today? How do you react to that evil?
3. What are your greatest weaknesses and strengths?
4. Is there anyone who tells you the truth about yourself? What is their relationship to you?

STUDY

Witnesses to the Truth

In John's Gospel, we are told that Jesus is the Word of God, the truth about God. Jesus tells us the truth about being human. God cannot lie, and Jesus confronts the whole world with the truth of what it claims to be and what it is not. Jesus was sent by God to bring light and life and truth to the world.

> He was in the world, and the world came to be through him, but the world did not know him. He came to what was his own, but his own people did not accept him. But to those who did accept him he gave power to become children of God.... The Word became flesh and made his dwelling among us, and we saw his glory, the glory as of the Father's only son, full of grace and truth.... From his fullness we have all received, grace in place of grace.
>
> John 1:10–12, 14, 16

We are the children of God—that is our truth—and God dwells with us. And he is "grace in place of grace" in our lives. That is our meaning as Christians. All of the choices we make, the deeds we perform, our relationships, are meant to reveal that truth for others: We are the children of God, with Jesus. We are words, small words, of God's glory and goodness, just as Jesus is the definitive Word—all there is to say about God in human terms. Each of us is called to speak something about God. No one else can say it. If we do not speak it and become it, then it is not said. It is like a piece of music and each of us is a note, or a pause between the notes. If we do not act like a child of God and speak clearly, then the note is off key, the song is sour. Jesus talks about this reality, about our relationship with God in the power of the Holy Spirit, with Nicodemus, a teacher who comes to see him at night. Jesus tells him (and us):

> Do not be amazed that I told you, "You must be born from above." The wind blows where it wills, and you can hear the sound it makes, but you do not know where it comes from or where it goes; so it is with everyone who is born of the Spirit.
>
> John 3:7–8

Jesus' Works as Testimony

But it is not just Jesus' words that testify to God and that witness to men and women about God's goodness and intent for the world. His actions are also witness: "These very works which I perform testify on my behalf that the Father has sent me." These works mark a Christian in the world. What are these works? In Luke's Gospel, Jesus says what he was sent to do:

> The Spirit of the Lord is upon me, because he has anointed me to bring glad tidings to the poor. He has sent me to proclaim liberty to captives and recovery of sight to the blind, to let the oppressed go free, to proclaim a year acceptable to the Lord.
>
> Luke 4:18–19

All of the choices we make, the deeds we perform, our relationships, are meant to reveal the truth that we are children of God in Jesus.

Jesus uses the words of the prophet Isaiah to describe his actions and what he will do with his life. His words and his works will tell the world what his Father is like and what he wants us to do and to be for one another.

At the Last Supper, he is still trying to get his friends, his disciples, to see him for who he is: the image of God that is clear and true. But they still don't see him with the eyes of faith. When he talks of his death and leaving them, Philip asks him: "Master, show us the Father, and that will be enough for us." And Jesus replies: "Have I been with you for so long and you still do not know me?" And he continues as clearly as he can:

> "Whoever has seen me has seen the Father. How can you say, 'Show us the Father'? Do you not believe that I am in the Father and the Father is in me? The words that I speak to you I do not speak on my own. The Father who dwells in me is doing his works. Believe me that I am in the Father and the Father is in me, or else, believe because of the works themselves. Amen, amen, I say to you, whoever believes in me will do the works that I do, and will do greater ones than these, because I am going to the Father. And whatever you ask in my name, I will do, so that the Father may be glorified in the Son.
>
> John 14:9–13

Each of us is called to speak something about God.

The Truth of Jesus

Jesus came to speak one truth, that God is our Father, and he promised his disciples in these words that if we believe in him we will do his works, and even do greater works! How? He will send us his Spirit, "the Spirit of truth, which the world cannot accept, because it neither sees nor knows it. But you know it, because it remains with you, and will be in you. I will not leave you orphans; I will come to you" (John 14:17–18).

We are never alone, the Spirit of Jesus dwells with us. This is what Etty Hillesum knew—that she was a dwelling place for God.

She looked for that dwelling place in every person she met, and she helped others make that dwelling place ready for God. This is the truth of who we are as Christians, and it is the reason for all our words, choices, and deeds.

The eighth commandment says, "Thou shalt not bear false witness against your neighbor." It means not only are we not to lie, slander, or perjure ourselves in court or in our dealings with others but we are not to witness to others anything that is not truthful. We are baptized and confirmed in witnessing to God in Jesus Christ. We must live with the truth that we are sinners and we do not live up to what we claim to be, and that we are called to worship God and obey him throughout our lives. We must live with the truth that the world does not accept Jesus as Lord or worship his Father and that evil must be confronted, both personally and collectively. We must live with the truth about our neighbors—that they image God no matter what is being done. It is up to us to find that image, encourage it, and relate to it, not to tear it down or harm it in any way. Of course, we are never to lie, never to keep silent in the face of evil, and never to let the truth go unspoken. But we are also to be careful of our words and actions that can betray who we are as the children of God.

The Spirit of Truth

The last gift of Jesus to his friends, to us, is his own Spirit, his own presence and strength in the Eucharist and in the gift of the Spirit. He gives himself and tells us to remember: "I have much more to tell you, but you cannot bear it now. But when he comes, the Spirit of truth, he will guide you to all truth." The eighth commandment reminds us that Jesus has left us his Spirit, who will lead us to the truth if we allow it. We must pray to be led by the Spirit and not just by our feelings or ideas. To lie in any way betrays that Spirit who has been given to us, the children of God, the children of the truth.

Witnesses to Christ

We are the children of God, baptized in his name and called to witness our belief and our reliance on God. The eighth commandment reminds us that our words and our actions, especially our moral choices, are to be clear indications, clear witnesses to the fact that we believe in God and in Jesus Christ. The word *testament,* as in the Old and New Testaments, means "last will," "desire," or "covenant" with those you love. The New Testament contains Jesus' will for his disciples, his way of living rightly and justly, his values and hopes for us as human beings and as friends of God our Father. We are asked to live up to and to try to imitate Jesus' ways of obeying God and being human. We witness to others who do not believe or who have trouble living up to Jesus' and the Church's standards more by our own actions than by any words that say we are Christians. Others watch us and see for themselves whether we are true to our words.

The Gift of Strength to Witness to God

It was the Spirit that enabled Jesus to stand up to the leaders of the Jews and the Romans and to preach his Father's kingdom of love, justice, and mercy, to forgive and to call others to repent of their old

We are asked to live up to and to try to imitate Jesus' ways of obeying God and being human.

ways and turn toward God and toward one another as children of the same Father. And that Spirit is given to us in Baptism and Confirmation so that we can rely on the grace and power of God to stand up for what we believe, in word and in deed.

In the baptismal ritual, there is a prayer that is offered for the newly baptized that states clearly what we are to do with the Spirit of God that is given to us:

> The promised strength of the Holy Spirit, which you are to receive, will make you more like Christ, and help you to be witnesses to his suffering, death and resurrection. It will strengthen you to be active members of the Church and to build up the Body of Christ in faith in love.
>
> (#229)

Then the celebrant lays hands on the newly baptized and asks for the power of the Spirit to come upon them. It is the same prayer offered at Confirmation.

> All powerful God, Father of our Lord Jesus Christ, by water and the Holy Spirit you freed your sons and daughters from sin and gave them new life. Send your Holy Spirit upon them to be their Helper and Guide. Give them the spirit of wisdom and understanding, the spirit of right judgment and courage, the spirit of knowledge and reverence. Fill them with the spirit of wonder and awe in your presence. We ask this through Christ our Lord. Amen.
>
> (#230)

Caught in the World

Etty Hillesum was no different than anyone else in Holland at the beginning of the Second World War. It took time for the new world to see what was happening, and a few courageous people spoke out against the killings of millions of people in concentration camps. Many who spoke out disappeared, and many never had a chance to speak. And yet, there are stories of men and women who—in the face of sure and inevitable death—spoke words of mercy, kindness, and forgiveness in spite of the bitterness and injustice of their own lives and what others were allowing to happen to them. Our words reveal our souls and what is most important to us. Our descriptions of other people, of what is happening, say that we believe in God, in forgiveness and hope, or that we no longer believe or only halfheartedly believe.

Etty's words changed as she did, as she grew in understanding and the wisdom of compassion. She learned that, no matter what happened, God was with his people and that it was possible to be like God in the midst of great suffering and persecution. For a believer in God, for those who call themselves Christian, this is the *truth*. This is the one truth, the only truth, we promise to proclaim by our lives when we are baptized. It is up to us to be clear about what we are saying with our lives. Others will look at us and know where we stand and what is important in our lives. We speak so loudly with our lives that what we are saying with our mouths often goes unheard.

Our Names, Our Words, Our Lives

At Confirmation we take another name, in honor or memory of someone who has lived up to their belief in Jesus in such a way that we wish to imitate them in our own lives. Our names are, in a sense, our word of honor. When we testify in a court of law or explain why we do something, it is our word of honor, our name, that carries the weight of what we say. Our namesake as Christians is Christ-bearer. We are to protect that name by our actions and by our standing with those who seek to live out their belief by right living and just moral choices. That is why we are Christians, members of the Church of Jesus, known by the company we keep as well as by our own individual lives and testimonies. The best testimony to our belief in Jesus as the Lord of our lives is to live up to his values and to choose freely to grow in his way of living. This is our truth in the deepest part of our person. We are first the children of God, called by name to show

WHAT ABOUT YOU?

1. What is the hardest thing about telling the truth in public?
2. Who is someone in your life who always tells the truth? What is their life like?
3. What actions can be lies?
4. Prayer is telling the truth about ourselves and God. How is prayer a part of the positive responses of the eighth commandment?

SCRIPTURE ACTIVITY

Do You Believe in Me?

The following Scripture passages have to do with Jesus' experiences of the truth with other people. Read the passages and write down what each of the people did and how they either betrayed the truth or stood up for it.

SCRIPTURE	ACTION	UPHELD OR BETRAYED TRUTH
John 18:15–17		
John 18:25–27		
Luke 23:13–25		
Luke 22:1–5		
Mark 14:48–50		
Mark 15:37–41		

SCRIPTURE ACTIVITY

I Do Believe!

Look up the following Scripture passages to see what it means to speak the truth as a follower of Jesus. What do each of these people do or say? What do these readings call us to do or say?

SCRIPTURE	ACTION	MESSAGE FOR US
Mark 16:9–11		
Mark 15:21		
Mark 6:30–33		
Mark 6:7–13		
Matthew 3:1–12		
Luke 1:46–55		

GROUP ACTIVITY

The Whole Truth and Nothing but the Truth

List some of the things that are difficult to stand up for in front of others (peer pressure) that you really do believe in. State where you stand on these issues and what would help you to be more truthful in saying and doing what you really believe about them. (*Suggestions*: cheating, stealing, cursing, talking about others, lying, drugs, drinking, pre-marital sex, birth control, abortion, smoking, fighting, grudges, exclusion of certain people from your group, rigging games, picking on one person, threats)

ISSUE	WHERE I STAND	HELPS IN TRUTH

Discerning the Truth

Choose a story from a newspaper or magazine that reports something you think is not true. Analyze the article by using the following outline. Then share your article with someone else.

What the article says:

What you don't believe—and why:

What the article says about us as human beings:

What you think is the truth of the matter:

What you think God would have to say about the article's truth:

7 The Greatest Commandment:
Love

PREPARATION PAGE

How Do I Love Thee?

1. Besides your family, who would you like to live with? Why?

2. To what "peoples" do you belong?

3. List all the meanings you've heard people use for the word *love*. What is the connection for each of these meanings to sexuality?

READING ACTIVITY

The l'Arche Community

Jean Vanier tells of his first meeting with mentally handicapped people and the effect it had on him. He entered the Canadian Navy at the age of thirteen during the Second World War. All of his education and training was geared toward efficiency. But when Vanier was stationed on the aircraft carrier *Magnificent* in 1950, he resigned his commission, inspired by the Gospel and the call to work for peace. He went to live in France in a community where people lived simply, studied philosophy and theology, prayed together, and discussed their beliefs and how to live them in the modern world. After he graduated, he went back to Canada and began teaching in St. Michael's College at the University of Toronto.

In 1963, Vanier was invited to visit Trosly-Breuil in France, a residence for thirty men with mental handicaps. Suddenly, everything seemed upside down. When he taught in Toronto, everyone was impressed by and interested in his information and learning, his degrees and his thoughts. Here in France, his new students weren't very interested in information, but they really wanted to know *him*, what he did, liked, believed, why he lived as he did, and they kept asking him when he would come back to see them again.

The men were simple, honest, emotional, sometimes hard to deal with, understand, and even be around, but they also still had the values of Jesus alive in them: love, kindness, singleheartedness, delight, child-likeness. Without really knowing what he was getting into, Jean Vanier took two handicapped men, Philippe and Raphael, from an insane asylum and had them move in with him. This was the beginning of what is today called l'Arche. Everyone who came to live at l'Arche (and there are now over seventy l'Arche communities and 200 houses) had to concentrate on making peace in their home.

All the houses begin with a concentration on structure, organization, and authority. Then—when there is some sense of security and acceptance, concentration on listening, and caring for people individually and helping each to grow and learn—each house eventually becomes a home, like a small family.

Support of others, friendship, community discipline, prayer, and ideas on how to use energies and discover ways to express love and affection help best to teach someone the meaning of sexuality and love. There is suffering, anguish, anger, lack of hope, and frustration at times, for anyone who really honestly looks at who they are in terms of their sexuality and how they are to love others. One thing is most true: Sexuality is never separated from love and compassion, from a relationship with the other person that is based on their good. Honesty, trust, forgiveness, and patience is where community begins and always returns. Jean Vanier knows this, and he says, "Growth begins when we start to accept our own weaknesses." And authority is necessary to help others to face who they are and to examine what is getting in the way of what they want to become. Authority is a responsibility for others, and that makes the one in authority alone. Authority cannot be compromised, and the truth must always be upheld and lived so that others can see the truth and follow it.

Vanier's time in l'Arche communities has given him moments of joy and courage and a sense that God lives and dwells with us in our brokenness. He tells a story of taking a group of handicapped men and women to the beach, the first time many of them had ever been there. After hours of walking along the edge of the water while collecting shells and watching the waves come in, one of them started drawing a huge circle on the beach. The water kept washing part of it away. Over and over and over again it was drawn. The man had infinite patience. Finally, someone went over to him and asked what he was doing. The man replied, "I'm trying to make enough room for joy."

Community, friendship, and love that is expressed with discipline and purity make enough room for joy in the heart of any person. Jean Vanier has learned and is trying to share with others the meaning of the greatest of the commandments: Thou shalt love the Lord your God with all your heart and all your soul and all your mind and all your strength; and the second half is like this: you shall love your neighbor as yourself, or with all your heart and all your soul and all your mind and all your strength. This kind of love demands control, care about others, and self-discipline. This is the kind of love Jesus asks of his disciples.

THINK IT OVER

1. How do mentally handicapped people make you feel? Do you know why?
2. What is your greatest "handicap," or weakness?
3. If you don't agree, what is it that you reject and why?

STUDY

Abide in My Love

Jesus' words to his disciples are very clear: "As the Father loves me, so I also love you. Remain in my love. . . . This is my commandment: love one another as I love you. No one has greater love than this, to lay down one's life for one's friends" (John 15:9, 12–13). Love is the basic requirement for the life of a Christian. But it is love as God envisions it, not as the media use it. It is love that sees rightly that we belong to God first, and it is that relationship that teaches us how to express affection, love, and tenderness to one another.

Being a Christian is tough, but we have the tenderness of God to rely on and to help us out. The essence of love is not found in sexuality but in friendship, compassion, and forgiveness. Only one kind of love is revealed in sexuality: love that is felt and sometimes shared by two people, love that is sensual and rooted in our bodies, love that physically connects us to people. But we must have a relationship that holds that connection in our hearts and souls for it to be true love. We must be careful of the other person and make sure that their best interests are at least as important as what we feel or want for ourselves. We all have the need to express affection and care for others, but learning to do that is an art that takes time, study, care, and discipline. Sexuality, especially genital sexuality, bonds us to another. If there is no friendship, no relationship of love already there, there is only selfishness, callousness, and usefulness—in other words, violence done to the body and soul of another person.

Being a Christian is tough, but we have the tenderness of God to rely on and to help us out.

Sexuality and Affection

Sexuality is how we express to others in the world the love that God shares with us. We must be very careful that what we express is *love* and not just our pleasure or our need or desire to have control over another. True love, we are told in Paul's Letter to the Corinthians, entails much more than feelings or expressing those feelings in sexuality.

> But I will show you a still more excellent way. If I speak in human and angelic tongues, I am a resounding gong or a clashing cymbal. And if I have the gift of prophecy, and comprehend all mysteries and all knowledge; if I have all faith so as to move mountains, but do not have love, I am nothing. If I give away everything I own, and if I hand my body over so that I may boast, but do not have love, I gain nothing.
>
> Love is patient, love is kind. It is not jealous, love is not pompous, it is not inflated, it is not rude, it does not seek its own interests, it is not quick-tempered, it does not brood over injury, it does not rejoice over wrongdoing but rejoices with the truth. It bears all things, believes all things, hopes all things, endures all things.
>
> Love never fails. . . . When I was a child, I used to talk as a child, think as a child, reason as a child; when I became a man, I put aside childish things. At present we see indistinctly, as in a mirror, but then face to face. At present I know partially; then I shall know fully as I am fully known. So faith, hope and love remain, these three; but the greatest of these is love.
>
> 1 Corinthians 13:1–13

This greatest of the commandments says that we are to love one another as we love God. That means we must be careful in our dealings with others and not betray our love for God in our relationships by being selfish, using others, taking care of our own needs and desires, or not truly caring about the person we are with.

Purity of Heart

"Purity of heart is to will one thing." This statement by Søren Kierkegaard is a good place to being to talk about purity. Another word for purity is *singlehearted*, desiring only one thing. For Christians, this purity is to desire only to love God and to love our neighbor as ourselves. To love God purely is to love God for himself alone, because he is God, and he is good and deserving of love and worship. To love our neighbors is to love them as we love ourselves, to act toward them as we would have others act toward us if we were in their same position. Native Americans say it this way: "Walk a mile in another man's mocassins and then you will know how to judge him and love him."

To be pure entails intention and desire, and then the discipline to act on that desire. The discipline of purity comes from prayer, from the support of a community that encourages us to live up to our ideals, and from friends who help us and stand by us and do not let us slide when the way gets rough.

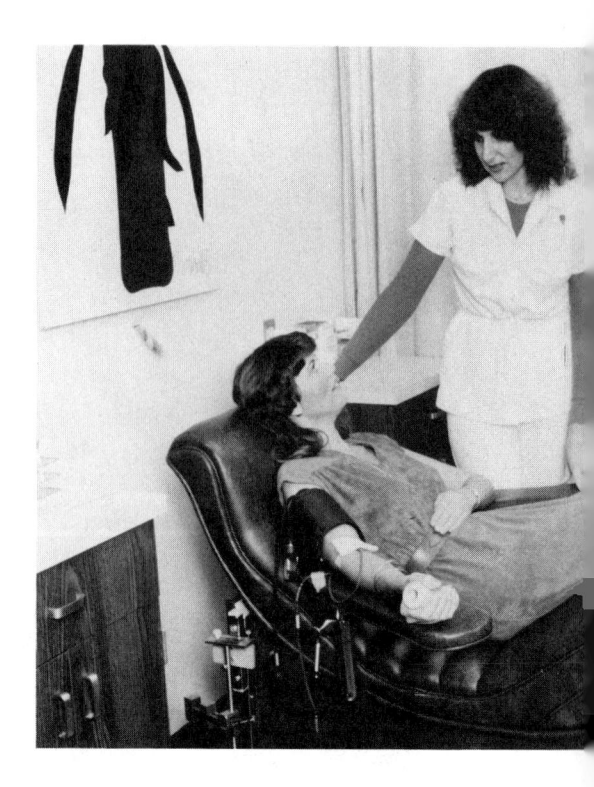

Community Prayer and Support

To yoke together has a number of meanings. When farmers wanted to plow a field they yoked oxen or horses together, and the two could do work that neither could do individually. The burden was split and shared. But to yoke together also carries the sense of the dancers as in the movie *Zorba the Greek*, when the men linked arms over one another's shoulders and danced together. Our burden of following Jesus and living up to his standards of love is easier when we share it with others, when we pray together, ask for help, have good friends, and act together for strength and solidarity. This is the meaning of community. We need to have groups of people who believe as we believe and who help us to live up to our beliefs in the presence of ridicule, peer pressure, and human weakness.

Jean Vanier's communities, the assistants who choose to live in community and the handicapped men and women they live with, have to learn to share one another's burdens as well as their joys. There is shared prayer, shared ideals, and shared rules and authority. Everyone freely chooses to obey the rules and regulations because they have been proven to be reliable in the past. When there are failures or infractions of the rules, there is discipline, forgiveness, and penance. There must be action as well as words to make up and to try to change what has happened for the better.

Vanier speaks of the authority of a person who calls the members of the community to honest and sincere relationships and who both encourages and calls them to account for their attitudes and behavior on a regular basis. All people who follow Jesus follow his authority over them. They obey his commandments and calls to conversion and a new way of living: forgiving, healing, helping one another, and being compassionate. But to obey Jesus, one often has to obey others who call us to account for our lives. A community helps us to see ourselves as we really are and not just as we want to see ourselves. It is a group of friends committed to one another in the spirit of Jesus.

Our burden of following Jesus and living up to his standards of love is easier when we share it with others.

The Suffering of Love

To love one another as Jesus has loved us and to lay down our lives for our friends is not an easy way to live. But Jesus tells us that this is his basic commandment and that all the others just make this one more apparent and precise. Suffering can mean plain difficulty in living up to what we know we are to do in public, or being thought crazy, or being ridiculed, or just going it alone and having to believe that what we are doing is right, even though it is difficult. But suffering is a part of life, and just as we are willing to put time, energy, and effort into what we want to do—for example, in running or swimming—we have to be willing to strive and discipline ourselves to follow God, too. If we play any sport, we know that we just can't play the game; we have to practice with the team, watch what we eat and when we sleep, and make certain that our attitude is one of positive support and affirmation of those with whom we play. This is the discipline of a community, and we need it if we are going to try to live up to the ideals of Jesus in loving one another and expressing affection, kindness, charity, and care for others, all others.

Service to Others

Vanier's community is based on living with, working with, and loving handicapped men and women that society would rather institutionalize. But Vanier and his friends know and believe that simple human kindness, charity, and care can help people to grow, even in the most difficult situations. Their service and simple acceptance of the handicapped adults brings hope and the possibility of friendship and understanding that would otherwise be lost to them. This element of service, charity, and kindness is crucial for all Christians to practice.

There is an ancient Christian hymn that says: "Where charity and love abide, there God is also found." Jesus told his disciples that, where two or three are gathered in his name, he is present there, too. And at the Last Supper in John's Gospel, Jesus washes his disciples' feet and tells them that they must do the same to one another, because he is a model for them. We are called to serve one another, especially those who are in need of service and kindness: the elderly, the sick, the isolated, the handicapped, the lonely, the single-parent family, the outsider in our family, parish, school, or local community. It is in providing companionship and support, as well as basic services, that each of us learns to love as Jesus did.

This kind of love is directed to more than just our friends and relatives and those we are supposed to love. It is given to anyone, but especially to those who need it and need us to give them affection, affirmation, support, and help. Each of us needs to belong to a group that reaches out to others in need: St. Vincent de Paul Society, visitors to the elderly and sick in nursing homes and hospitals, or Big Brother and Big Sister programs. Other groups that reach out include soup kitchens or any other group that works to make the lives of others richer and more human by their love and help.

We are called to serve one another, especially those who are in need of service and kindness.

Affection and Love

Adolescence is a time of learning to express our feelings of affection, anger, care, fear, insecurity, hope, and so on. It is not an easy time, but it is a time of energy and promise. Our relationships with our families undergo many changes and each of us experiments with how to say we care about someone, whether it be emotional feelings, physical gestures of affection or anger, or just how to cope with frustration and sexual needs. It is a time when we need friends and groups and many different kinds of relationships to help us learn how to say who we are as individuals. The only way to learn how to express feelings is by trial and error, so it is best to practice in contexts where there are boundaries and guidelines and support from others who have also had to learn and are still maturing as human beings and as Christians. Many of the service groups also pray together and talk about the feelings that work and service cause in us. In this context, it is easier to learn and be more honest with our feelings. There are also rules to know and follow so that the first care is for those we have come to serve.

We Are Christ on Earth

This greatest commandment, to love as God has loved us, calls us to be careful of others so that we do not always put our needs and wants ahead of others. It is a commandment not to be selfish. God dwells within us through our baptism, and our bodies are meant to be used as the medium through which we manifest God and share the love he has given us with others. We bear Christ in our bodies, and we take him to others and receive him from others. This commandment is the fulfillment of all the others: When we love others rightly, then we love God; and if we truly love God, then we will be careful with them as we would be with God standing before us. Saint Teresa of Avila had this in mind when she wrote this prayer:

> Christ has no body now on earth but yours. No hands but yours. No feet but yours. Yours are the eyes through which must look out Christ's compassion on the world. Yours are the feet with which he is to go about doing good. Yours are the hands with which he is to bless people now.

Through our sexuality and our love, we are Christ to one another. That is what this commandment tells us to remember when we say we love someone.

WHAT ABOUT YOU?

1. How do prostitution, pornography, masturbation, and genital sexuality outside of marriage betray the love we are told to extend to others?
2. You are Christ to others. How can you use your sexuality to express the kind of love that Jesus gave to others?
3. When you make a mistake and betray God's love, what does the Gospel say that Jesus will do?
4. What do you think it means to "be singlehearted and pure"?
5. How do you know that "you have loved much" so that you will "be forgiven much"?

SCRIPTURE ACTIVITY

Failure and Forgiveness

What if you are struggling with right use of your sexuality and you fail? How will God treat you and what does he ask you to do? Look up the following stories in Scripture and write down what Jesus says he will do for you and what you must do in return.

SCRIPTURE	WHAT JESUS WILL DO	WHAT I MUST DO IN RETURN
Luke 15:1–7		
Luke 15:8–10		
Luke 15:11–32		
Luke 13:6–9		
Matthew 7:12–14		
Matthew 8:1–4		

SCRIPTURE ACTIVITY

The Pure in Heart

What does it mean to be pure in heart? Look up the following passages to see what the Scriptures say. List what you need to be and do to be pure.

SCRIPTURE	WHAT I MUST DO TO BE PURE
Matthew 13:44–46	
Matthew 25:1–12	
Matthew 26:36–44	
Luke 1:38	
Luke 2:19	
John 14:23	

GROUP ACTIVITY

Discipline in My Life

PART I

The following is a list of the twelve fruits of the Holy Spirit. Next to each of them, fill in a behavior that you think is opposite to the gift or virtue.

FRUIT OF THE HOLY SPIRIT	OPPOSITE BEHAVIOR
Charity	
Joy	
Peace	
Patience	
Kindness	
Goodness	
Long suffering (endurance)	
Gentleness	
Faith	
Truthfulness	
Self-control	
Chastity	

PART II

Next to each of the fruits of the Holy Spirit write down two ways to use this fruit to express or discipline your life in the area of sexuality.

FRUIT OF THE HOLY SPIRIT	APPLICATION FOR SEXUALITY
Charity	
Joy	
Peace	
Patience	
Kindness	
Goodness	
Long suffering (endurance)	
Gentleness	
Faith	
Truthfulness	
Self-control	
Chastity	

8 The Beatitudes:
Justice

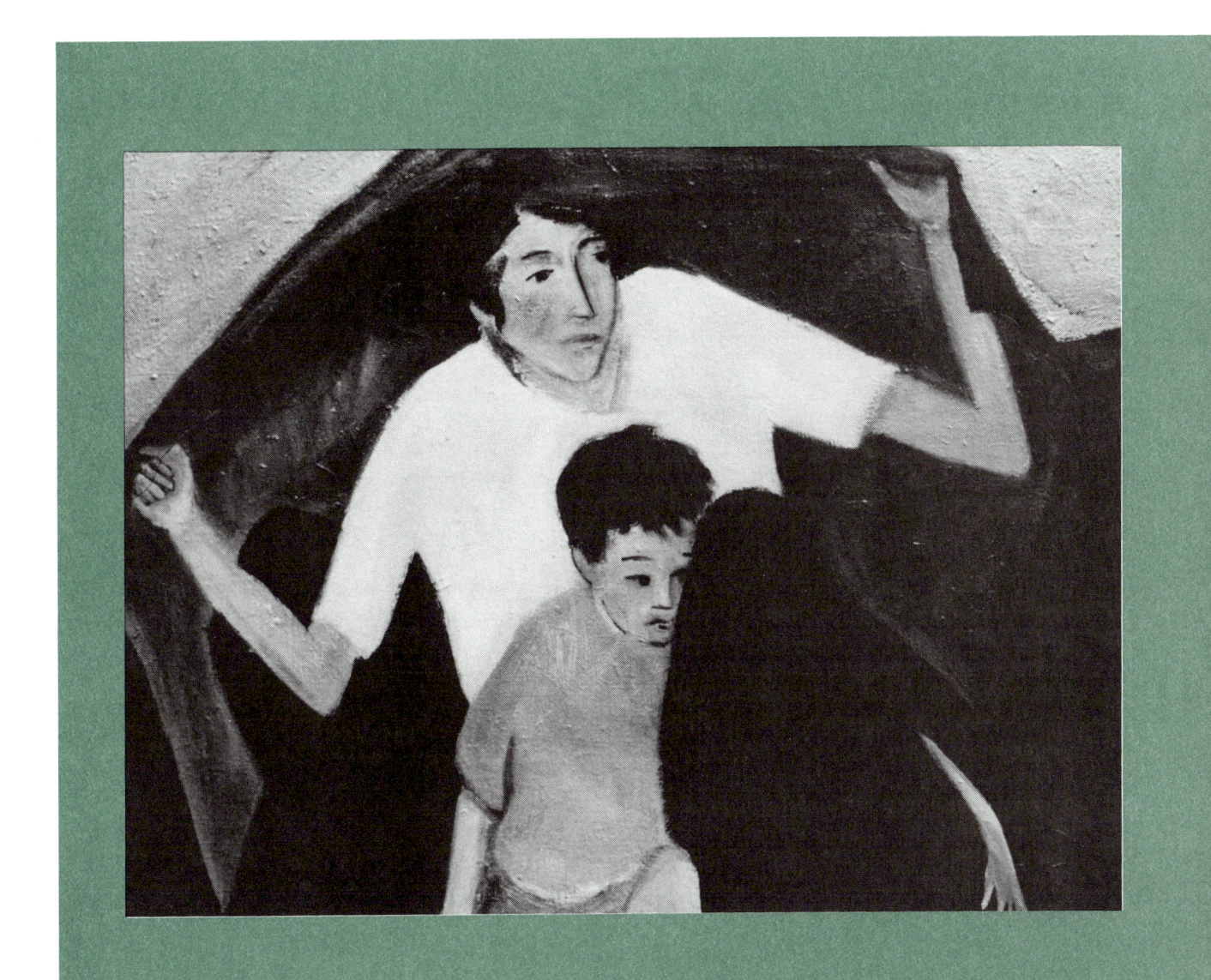

PREPARATION PAGE

Justice and Mercy for All

1. When you die, do you want God to deal mercifully or justly with you? Why?

2. When have you shown mercy to others?

3. What do you think the words "justice for all" mean?

READING ACTIVITY

We Can Change Our Lives

> The stone suffers because all speak of its hardness and yet you used to look for a stone as a pillow for your head, for you knew and you know that the hope of stones is to serve. When they serve they become as soft as clouds.

These words were written ten years ago by a man named Dom Helder Camara, the archbishop of Recife, Brazil. He goes on:

> Have you ever seen a dry sponge full of chalk dust? Have you ever held in your hand a dry sponge stiff with chalk? If you dip it in water, all the hardness disappears, all the stiffness vanishes. When I meet hearts that are like sponges stiff with chalk, how I would like to plunge them into the water of God's infinite goodness!
>
> One day a lady, a dear friend of mine, said to me: "I'd be quite happy if my heart were like a sponge stiff with chalk. My case is worse. My heart has turned to stone. What good is a petrified heart?"
>
> There are moments when words come to us that we did not know we had, unforeseen words, breathed directly into us by the Spirit of God. I repeated her words and commented on them: "What good is your heart that has turned to stone? It's marvelous! Magnificent! Christ says he does not have even a stone on which to lay his head. Offer him your 'stone.'"
>
> The next day my friend said to me: "Yesterday evening your words about Jesus not having even a stone on which to lay his head made me say to him: 'I find this a bit awkward. But if it's true that you are looking for a stone on which to lay your head, well, I have my stone here. It's a real joy for me to serve you, even in such a poor way.'"
>
> And she continued: "I had an utterly deep sleep—something very rare for me. And the next day my heart no longer felt like a stone. I could look at everyone—even those who hate me and do me evil and are paid back with even stronger hate from me—I could look at everyone and almost sing for joy and peace." Where has the pessimism gone? The cold, dead questions; where are they? The "What good is it? What good is it?" Let us keep hoping! We can change our lives, transform our hearts.
>
> (From *Hoping Against All Hope*, [Maryknoll, N.Y.: Orbis Books, 1974] pp. 9–10)

Dom Helder is a bishop in his late seventies, the leader of one of the largest and poorest dioceses in northeastern Brazil. He has been the bishop there since 1964, and in 1986, he retired, although he still resides in the same area of the slum. Recife is the capital of the State of Pernambuco in the northeast region of Brazil. People descended from three continents dwell there: Africa, Europe, and Amerindian nations. It is the world of the poor in the midst of a teeming society of luxury hotels. It is the home of the security of the rich and the mud of the millions of poor.

For twenty years, the military was in power in Brazil, and any group that offered resistance or outcry was silenced. At the least suspicion, teachers, workers, college students, journalists, and politicians faced arrest, torture, prison, and death. But the Church stood with the people, organizing and supporting them, speaking on their behalf, campaigning for civil and human rights, and preaching a theology of freedom for all, human dignity, and liberation from oppression, fear, and inhuman poverty. Dom Helder was the leader and the model of the Church during that time. He was physically threatened; his friends were attacked; journalists were not permitted to mention his name or quote his words. But he preached "good news to the poor" nonetheless. His reputation is one of holiness and care for the poor people of his parish: all of northeastern Brazil, and some say, all of Latin America.

This bishop, known and respected by so many people and feared and disrespected by so many in power, has been called dangerous, a child, simpleminded, a saint, the voice of those who have no voice, a poet, a prophet, and the defender of those who nonviolently struggle for justice in South America.

A Thousand Reasons for Living is the title of one of Dom Helder's books of poetry. It is a collection of his nightly meditations, his radio sermons, his musings, and his words to the people he lives with and works for justice with. It is also a litany of hope and gratitude, a thousand reasons to praise God's goodness and intent in creating us and sharing his life with us.

Dom Helder Camara believes and acts out of one belief alone: All men and women were meant to live as brothers and sisters, equal and free as God created them, and Jesus Christ's message of "good news for the poor, sight to the blind, hope to the brokenhearted, release to prisoners, a year of favor from the Lord" (Luke 4) is meant to be a reality in our churches and countries. His dream of justice is not an impossible one, just one that is hard and demanding yet worth living for with others. He is recognized the world over as the strongest voice of the Third World (the poorest nations on earth) for justice, responsible economics, and the nonviolent struggle for human rights.

THINK IT OVER

1. How do you think Dom Helder Camara is different from other bishops you know?
2. What do you think bishops do for people? What kinds of things do you think they should do?
3. Dom Helder is known for his work for justice. What do you think the work of justice entails?

STUDY

The Power of the Bible's Message

In the Book of Exodus, we read about the beginnings of freedom and how God called his people out of bondage and into a promised land of peace. It is the universal story of the struggle for justice and human dignity.

> Then a new king, who knew nothing of Joseph, came to power in Egypt. He said to his subjects, "Look how numerous and powerful the Israelite people are growing, more so than we ourselves! Come, let us deal shrewdly with them to stop their increase, otherwise, in time of war they too may join our enemies to fight against us and so leave our country." Accordingly taskmasters were set over the Israelites to oppress them with forced labor. Thus they had to build for Pharoah the supply cities of Pithom and Raames. Yet the more they were oppressed, the more they multiplied and spread. The Egyptians, then, dreaded the Israelites and reduced them to cruel slavery, making life bitter for them with hard work in mortar and brick and all kinds of field work—the whole cruel fate of slaves.
>
> Exodus 1:8–14

The God of the Bible is the God of freedom and justice. He hears the cry of his people in bondage and has compassion on them and their suffering. He says to Moses:

> "I have witnessed the affliction of my people in Egypt and have heard their cry of complaint against their slave-drivers, so I know well what they are suffering. . . . The cry of the Israelites has reached me, and I have truly noted that the Egyptians are oppressing them. Come, now! I will send you to Pharoah to lead my people, the Israelites, out of Egypt."
>
> Exodus 3:7–10

God is witness in the Old Testament to what goes on in the world, and nothing goes unheeded, certainly not injustice and suffering. God is the God of liberation and hope, who interferes and works with people in history to change the world into what it was created to be: a home and not a place of slavery or a prison of hopelessness and injustice.

The Long Story

The entire Old Testament is the dialogue of God with his people, calling them to act like him and promising that he will send one who is so just and so compassionate that all will know that God dwells with them. Jesus himself uses the prophecies of Isaiah to describe who he is and what his message of good news is all about.

> I, the Lord, have called you for the victory of justice, I have grasped you by the hand; I formed you, and set you as a covenant of the people, a light for the nations, to open the eyes of the blind, to bring out prisoners from confinement, and from the dungeon, those who live in darkness.
>
> Isaiah 42:6–7

As Christians, as followers and disciples of Jesus, we believe that Jesus is the Messiah, the long-awaited and heralded presence of God with his people, who is justice and peace for all who believe in him. Jesus is the Savior of the world, liberating and freeing us from sin, injustice, and all evil of body and soul. Jesus often preaches forgiveness, and then heals the bodies as well as the souls and spirits of the people, so that they can see his power of love and compassion for them. Matthew describes the work of Jesus: "[Jesus] went around all of Galilee, teaching in their synagogues, proclaiming the gospel of the kingdom, and curing every disease and illness among the people" (Matthew 4:23). And during the week of his death, as he comes into the city of Jerusalem, where all the prophets of God met their deaths, the people cry out: "Blessed is he who comes in the name of the Lord!" (Mark 11:10).

The Incarnation

Jesus in one of us. He has known our joy in living, our sufferings, and our deaths. Loving us, he shows us how to live by dwelling with us and teaching us what it means to be human and to be like God. This is our belief in the Incarnation: that Jesus, the Christ, the Son of God, is human and like us in all things but sin, loving us as his own brothers and sisters, his friends, and loving us so much that he would share our suffering and death. He would be with us in all things. The justice of God, the kingdom of Jesus' Father, is based on the Incarnation—that God loves us tenderly as his children and sends his own beloved Child to be our comfort and strength and model for living and dying.

Justice

The dictionary defines *justice* as "being righteous," "fairness," "rightfulness," "reward or penalty deserved," "the use of authority to uphold what is just," "the administration of law," and "to treat fairly or with due appreciation." But that is justice on earth, among people and governments. The justice of God, as described by the prophets and preached by Jesus, entails "being righteous" and much more. The words for justice also mean holiness, righteousness, and tenderness. The fourth Beatitude of Jesus, "Blessed are they who hunger and thirst for righteousness," begins to reveal what God means by justice. Because we are to "hunger and thirst" for this, the understanding of justice has a great deal to do with food and drink, the basic necessities of life.

Governments and international groups, such as the United Nations, acknowledge that justice is the basic right of all peoples to food, clothing, shelter, medicine, education, human dignity, and freedom. Yet the worldwide statistics presented in the *National Catholic Reporter* of December 12, 1986, are grim and terrible:

1. Every sixty seconds, twenty-eight people die of hunger-related causes.
2. One child in ten dies before his or her first birthday.
3. In eighty-three countries, three percent of the landowners control eighty percent of the land.
4. Seventy percent of the world's people consume only ten percent of the world's resources.
5. Fifty percent of the world's people lack clean drinking water.
6. The developing nations now owe more than eight hundred billion dollars, two-thirds of the money due to banks in the United States.
7. Fifty percent of the world's hungry live in only five countries—India, Bangladesh, Nigeria, Pakistan, and Indonesia. Africa is the poorest continent.
8. Between 340 million and 900 million people in the world are malnourished. One sixth of the people in eighty-seven developing countries will have serious health problems as a result of an inadequate diet.

And these statistics do not even mention the fact that the United States comprises six percent of the world's population and yet consumes over sixty percent of the world's resources. Still, twenty-five percent of the children in the United States are malnourished. All of these numbers say only one thing: The world is always hungry. The majority of people in the world hunger and thirst for food—and justice.

There are two statements of Dom Helder Camara that have been quoted extensively in the last twenty years. They are: "There is enough for the world's need, but not for the world's greed" and "When I fed the poor they called me a saint and when I asked why the poor were hungry, they called me a communist." The issue of hunger is one of economics and justice, as well as one of charity and religion. The commandment of love calls us to feed the hungry. It is not an option. We read in Matthew's Parable of the Sheep and the Goats that we will be judged by whether or not we have practiced the corporal works of mercy while we have lived. It is blunt and demanding, because those who gain the kingdom of heaven often don't realize who they are helping and treating as their neighbor and their friends. But Jesus' Beatitudes, as found in Matthew and Luke, are made very specific in these words:

> "Lord, when did we see you hungry or thirsty or a stranger or naked or ill or in prison, and not minister to your needs?" He will answer them, "Amen I say to you, what you did not do for one of these least ones, you did not do for me."
>
> Matthew 25:44–45

Jesus is interested in more than laws and what is required by governments or nations. It is the spirit of the law that must be lived

> When I fed the poor they called me a saint and when I asked why the poor were hungry, they called me a communist.

and practiced. Justice is the right of every human being, and to work for and to struggle with those who work for justice is to bring the kingdom that Jesus preached as good news. To work for the reality of everyone sharing in the basic necessities of life—food, clothing, shelter, medicine, education, human dignity, and freedom—is to work for the coming of the kingdom of heaven here on earth, as Jesus did.

The Beatitudes

In the Sermon on the Mount, Jesus gives a guideline for living as a disciple that involves action and work for justice as well as a personal conversion and life-style, which begins with changes in our attitudes. The Beatitudes are just that: attitudes of being, ways of being a Christian, so the world knows what our values are through our words, actions, and priorities in the world. The first four Beatitudes highlight the values of justice.

> Blessed are the poor in spirit
>   for theirs is the kingdom of heaven.
> Blessed are they who mourn,
>   for they will be comforted.
> Blessed are the meek,
>   for they will inherit the land.
> Blessed are they who hunger and thirst for righteousness
>   for they will be satisfied.
>   Matthew 5:3–6

The Beatitudes are just that: attitudes of being, ways of being Christian.

The listing of the Beatitudes in Luke (where there are only four, with four curses as well) makes very clear that they are concerned as much with existence on earth as in the spirit or the soul of people.

> Blessed are you who are poor,
>   for the kingdom of God is yours.
> Blessed are you who are now hungry,
>   for you will be satisfied.
> Blessed are you who are now weeping,
>   for you will laugh.
> Blessed are you when people hate you, and when they exclude
>   and insult you, and denounce your name as evil on account
>   of the Son of Man.
>   Rejoice and leap for joy on that day! Behold, your reward
>   will be great in heaven. For their ancestors treated the
>   prophets in the same way.
>
> But woe to you who are rich,
>   for you have received your consolation.
> But woe to you who are filled now,
>   for you will be hungry.
> Woe to you who laugh now,
>   for you will grieve and weep.
> Woe to you when all speak well of you,
>   for their ancestors treated the false prophets in this way.
>   Luke 6:20–26

The practice of the Beatitudes aligns us with the tradition of Jesus who fed the hungry, healed the sick, gave hope and comfort to outcasts, and died as a political and religious prisoner. God's justice is revealed in the tender, loving kindness of Jesus, who shares our suffering and shows us how to live in the face of injustice and unnecessary suffering. His commandment is to right injustice and to lift up the broken-hearted and to bring hope to those who are oppressed and without any power, except the power of love and trust in God. To be poor means to trust God and to freely share what we don't need so that others do not have to do without. It means to freely choose—like the rich young man refused to do—to go and sell what we have and give it to the poor and then, come and follow Jesus more closely. The commandment of justice demands that we share our wealth and our excess so that others may truly live with dignity as human beings.

The World as Our Neighborhood

The Beatitudes call us to look at the poor, the sorrowing, those who are meek (nonviolent or lowly), and those who hunger and thirst for justice for all. We are to side with them, to stand with them, and to live in solidarity with them. The majority of the world's people falls into these categories: the hungry, those who suffer persecution and injustice in dictatorships and free nations, the improvised, the immigrant, the alien, the prisoner, the sick, and the aged and infirm. The poor, we are told in the present tense, already have the kingdom

The commandment of justice demands that we share our wealth and our excess so that others may truly live with dignity as human beings.

of God with them. If we are to be a part of the kingdom of God now in our lives, we must be friends with the poor. We must try in our daily personal prayer and life-style to live simply, to be aware of our gifts and responsibilities, and to share with others who do not have as much as we need or even enough to survive.

In addition, we must realize that we are children of one earth, one planet that has been separated and divided into nations of haves and have nots. We belong to a universal Church and we have universal care for the world that was given to us to have dominion over and subdue. We are responsible for what we do with our natural resources: fuels, energies, food, land, and water. We have the responsibility to learn about world economics, politics, and food and land issues that are affected by national and international policies. We cannot be comfortable while others starve, wander without shelter, or are deprived of their freedoms.

Nonviolence

The Beatitudes are extremely clear about how this is to come about: by meek, lowly, peaceful, nonviolent methods and by people who practice these methods personally and collectively. This issue will be dealt with more extensively in the following chapter, where the last four Beatitudes and the commandment to mercy and peace is presented. We are the children of God, the disciples and friends of Jesus, and we are to imitate our God who is loving, compassionate, forgiving, slow to anger, truthful, not afraid to stand up for the poor and the needy, and not afraid to stand with them as friends. "See how they love one another," was the early Church's hallmark. They loved the widow, the orphan, the slave, the poor, the leper, and the illegal alien, and they cared for them as one of the family—because that's who they were by baptism and love.

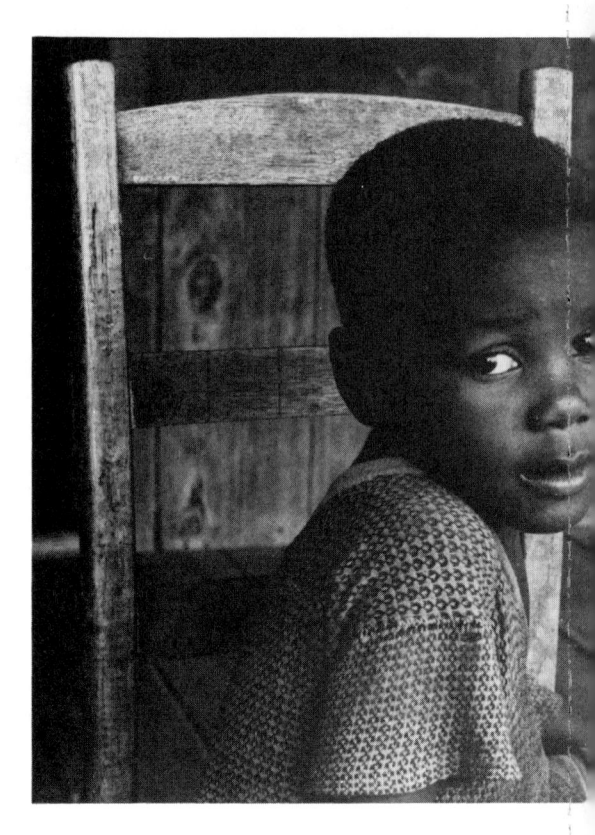

WHAT ABOUT YOU?

1. How does reading about the hunger problems of the world make you feel? How do you translate those feelings into action on behalf of others?
2. If you want God to deal with you justly, do you treat others with justice? Or, if you want God to deal with you mercifully, are you merciful to others?
3. Have you ever visited another country? What was it like for you as an American and as a Christian?

SCRIPTURE ACTIVITY

Economics, Land, and Religion

Read the story of King Ahab and Queen Jezebel in 1 Kings 21:1–16. Then answer the following questions.

1. Why didn't Naboth want to give or sell his land to the King and Queen?

   _____
   _____

2. What emotions and actions does Ahab the King show in the story?

   _____
   _____
   _____

3. What emotions and actions does Queen Jezebel show in the story?

   _____
   _____
   _____

4. What does the prophet Elijah do to Ahab and Jezebel? What is the punishment that he delivers to the King and Queen?

   _____
   _____
   _____

5. What are your feelings and reactions to this story and the lesson it teaches?

   _____
   _____
   _____

SCRIPTURE ACTIVITY

Mary's Prayer for Liberation

Read Mary's prayer for her people before Jesus is born, found in Luke 1:46–55. Then make a list of the things that God is doing and will do for his people. Then match your list with the four Beatitudes you have studied (found in Matthew 5:3–6 and in Luke 6:20–26).

GOD'S WORK	BEATITUDES
1.	
2.	
3.	
4.	
5.	
6.	
7.	
8.	
9.	
10.	

GROUP ACTIVITY

Present-day Pharisees

Read aloud Jesus' harsh words to the Pharisees found in Matthew 23:1–39. Below are listed the actions that Jesus condemns. After each name or action, write a contemporary example of the same thing.

ACTION	TODAY
Lay heavy burdens on people	
Perform works to be seen	
Love public honor	
Stress on money/tithing	
Importance of outward appearances	
Build monuments	
Persecute true prophets	

9 The Beatitudes:
Peace

PREPARATION PAGE

Peace on Earth, Good Will to All

1. Personally, what emotions do you associate with peace in your life?

2. What events do you associate with peace in the world?

3. Who is the most peaceful person you know personally and what are they like to be with?

4. Do you consider yourself a peacemaker? If so, what do you do to create peace in the world?

5. What do you think are the greatest threats to world peace?

READING ACTIVITY

In Solitary Witness

There is a small village in Upper Austria called Saint Radegund. A few miles north of this village lies Kreisstadt, Braunauam-Inn, the birthplace of Adolf Hitler. A few more miles north is the provincial capital of Linz, where Adolf Eichmann was raised. These small towns are remembered only because of three people who began their lives in obscurity and ended their lives having affected the whole world.

Hitler did more to destroy civilization by seeking to exterminate millions of people, the Jews being the most well-known group. The man who was his collaborator in this task, which Hitler called the Final Solution, was Eichmann, unrivaled for his brutality and cruelty. The third man, from the village of Saint Radegund, is not as well known, but it is to his village that those who seek peace and freedom and who rely on the power of the Spirit to stand against evil based on their own consciences continue to go. This man was Franz Jagerstatter.

Franz was the only person in Saint Radegund (and one of very few people in Germany or Austria) to refuse to legitimate an event and fact that had already happened politically. Hitler had achieved power in Germany. The Fuhrer and his new order, the "Thousand-year Reich," was a reality, and military service was inevitable for all. National Socialism was taking over every institution and organization, and Hitler's Youth were strong in their anti-religious doctrines and activities. But the Catholic Church of Austria was virtually silent. In fact, when Jagerstatter decided not to take the oath or to serve in the German Army, his own pastors and spiritual director pleaded with him to obey and not to follow his conscience.

It was not until August, 1983, that the bishop of Linz, the diocese where Saint Radegund is located, spoke on behalf of Franz's decision. He came to the village on the fortieth anniversary of Jagerstatter's death and celebrated Mass and preached in his honor. Bishop Aichern spoke of Jagerstatter as one man who understood completely what he was doing and what were the consequences that his one action would bring upon him and his family. Yet, "his faith and his conscience pointed the way that he must follow." Franz did not accuse those who registered and fought or those who remained silent in the face of what was happening. He was not even interested in convincing others to join him and to act with him. He was only attempting to be true to *his* conscience and what it demanded of him as a Christian.

Earlier in his life, however, there was no indication that he was any more religious than anyone else. In fact he was thought of as wild and reckless on occasion and the leader of his group. He was the first to have a motorcycle in the village, and he spent a few days in jail after a battle over his group's turf. He did leave the village for several years.

But sometime after his return to the village, he began to change the way he lived. He began to go to church daily and to receive the sacraments; he read the Bible in the fields; he sang and prayed the Psalms; and he began to stop the previous ways of spending and wasting his time. In 1937, he married a woman named Franziska, and they went on a honeymoon to Rome, an unusual choice for farmers in those days. Even today, his wife is "blamed" for his change and his eventual choice to refuse military service. That change was *not* seen as positive or attractive to his neighbors. After his refusal to sign the oath, imprisonment gave him time to read, pray, study and write down his thoughts, feelings, and reasons for his action, as well as to write about the Christian responsibility to make peace, to speak the truth, and to stand in opposition to any authority that is not true to life and freedom.

In one of his commentaries on the situation facing Catholics in the Third Reich, he wrote about a dream he had several years before, when the political order was just beginning to alter society in Germany and Austria. In his dream, he saw a splendid, shining train circling a mountain. Everyone, including the children, was rushing to get a place on the train. Then he heard a voice yelling a warning: "This train is going to Hell." He decided he was not going along on the ride. He wrote years later in prison, after he had made his choice to refuse to ride on the train:

> It is still possible for us, even today, to lift ourselves with God's help out of the mire in which we are stuck and win eternal happiness—if we only make a sincere effort and bring all our strength to the task. . . . It may well be that hell holds great power over this world at the present time, but even this need not cause us Christians to fear. May the power of hell be ever so great, God's power is still greater.

In his own words he spoke of his life: "I cannot and may not take an oath in favor of a government that is fighting an unjust war." It was his way of making peace a reality in the midst of hatred and war. That one action cost him his life and may bring him recognition one day as a saint in the Church.

THINK IT OVER NOW

1. What do you think about Franz Jagerstatter's refusal to sign the oath and to participate in the military?
2. If he lived today, how do you think you'd react to his decision? What would you say to him?
3. What do you understand "conscientious objection" to be for a Catholic?
4. If Franz Jagerstatter's action makes him a peacemaker, how can you become a peacemaker today?

STUDY

Peacemaking

The ideal of peace and the commandment to make peace underlie much of Jesus' own understanding of himself and his message. Jesus is the peace of God that arises from a long history of *shalom*, the Jewish concept of peace as a religious reality. A story from the Talmud, told of Aaron, the High Priest, illustrates peace as a practical life-style:

> When two people would have an argument, Aaron would go to one and say, "I heard your friend weeping, crying to himself, 'How could I have been so foolish as to damage my friendship? I would do anything to have my friend back.'" He would then go to the second one and say, "I overheard your friend weeping, crying to himself, 'What could possibly have been worth the anger I showed my friend? I would do anything to have his friendship back.'"
>
> The first would think to himself, "My friend can't be all bad if he is so distraught at what he said to me. I'll go and comfort him." And the second would say to himself, "My friend must truly be a good friend if he is so remorseful over his words to me. I'll go and comfort him." When they would meet on the street, on their way to one another, they would immediately embrace and once again be friends.

This story reveals the positive side of peace—not the absence of hate, war, or disharmony, but the intent to bridge differences, to go out of one's way to bring others together, to think kindly of them, and to reach out to both sides in any relationship or dispute.

The Dream of Peace

The prophets, especially Isaiah and Micah, sing and speak of peace. Their famous words seem an unbelievable reality, yet they are the basis of the coming of the Messiah: "And it shall come to pass in the days to come . . . that they shall beat their swords into plowshares and their spears into pruning hooks. Nation shall not lift up sword against nation, neither shall they learn war anymore" (Isaiah 2:2 and Micah 4:1). Others exhorted the people: "Love the truth and peace. Not by might nor by power, but by my spirit says the Lord of Hosts" (Zechariah 4:6).

The Choice for Life Is Peace

All these understandings of peace are based on the original choice of the Israelites to be the People of God, a light to the other nations. At the end of their passage through the desert, Moses confronts them. They are ready to enter the Promised Land after forty years of wandering in the desert. They have left Egypt, slavery, and hate behind and now call themselves the people of their God Yahweh. Moses reads to them their choice for the future: "I call heaven and earth to witness against you this day, that I have set before you life and death, the blessing and the curse, therefore choose life that both you and your descendants will live" (Deuteronomy 30:19). This line is still presented each year to the Jewish people on their New Year. Shalom is found in the act of choosing life, life for all, always and in every place. The God of the Jews is the God of life.

Creation and Shalom

In the beginning, we are told that when God looked at what he had created, he found it good. He was pleased with the earth and his children. The rabbis say that after God finished creating the trees and forests, the waters and the animals, he took Adam for a walk in the garden and told him, "See my works, how fine and excellent they are. All that I have created has been given to you. Remember this and do not corrupt and desolate my world, for if you corrupt it, there is no one after you to set it right." The Talmud of the Jewish people teaches that life is the ultimate reality and the principle of religion, of worship, and of relationships in the world. It teaches that one man alone was created (Adam) and one woman (Eve—the mother of all the living) to teach that one who destroys even one human soul is regarded as though he had destroyed the entire world. And if you save one human soul, then you save the whole world.

Repairing the World

But for the Jews there is more. God has left creation unfinished; he has given the earth to us and trusted us with continuing what he started. The sanctity of human life is the basic principle of all imagination and creativity, or progress and growth, and of being human. Our job is to complete the world, to apply the blessing and the practices of shalom to creation. We are to bring peoples into communion, unite opposing factions, break down barriers, pull together what is divided, and bring the world to completeness—to make it holy and pleasing to God. And we are to look at all peoples in the world as family, regardless of race, nationality, sex, creed, or political beliefs. These are the ancient teachings of the Jewish sages. Even the transformation of enemies is rooted in the concept of shalom. There is a saying: "Who is the greatest hero? One who changes an enemy into a friend."

This concept of peace is all-inclusive. God's name is peace and all other blessings, and all prayers are contained in the name of God. All these calls to peace are situated in the harsh reality of human beings and in the continuing presence of hate, fear, insecurity, inhumanity, murder, and war among human beings.

One who destroys even one human soul is regarded as though he had destroyed the entire world. And if you save one human soul, then you save the whole world.

Life and Death

The issues of hate, jealousy, fear, and difference begin early in the story of humanity. In Genesis, the story is told of the first two children of Adam and Eve: Cain and Abel. These are the first children, and each of us has a portion of Cain and a portion of Abel is us. Each of us is capable of murdering our brothers and sisters, and we are reminded of it so that we can face it squarely and deal with those tendencies to sin: to kill life, to destroy hope, to eliminate fear and insecurity by attacking others. The great sins are the sins against peace: killing, maiming, torturing, starving, imprisoning, excluding, hating, vengeance, jealousy, rage, abuse, and making enemies of others. Genesis tells about the beginnings of our relationship with God and how we live with one another.

God's Questions to Us

In Genesis, God asks us two questions. The first is "Where are you?" Where are you in relation to me? Are you hiding from me? And the second is "Where is your brother?" Are you still connected? Are you being responsible for life? Are you being truthful? Are you being and allowing others to be? Cain responds, "Am I my brother's keeper?" God's very question says clearly, "Yes, you are." We are human beings created in the image and likeness of God, and we are to create life, to imitate God. We are inhuman or not human when we treat any life with antipathy, indifference, or lack of respect.

Jesus' Message of Peace

The commandment to make peace, to be peace, and to pray for peace is based on Jesus' person, his life, death, and resurrection. Jesus is our peace. Peace is always a gift from God, as is life itself. It is connection with God. The covenant of the Old Testament is a bonding of peace—peace between God and his people. Ezekiel says, "God will establish an everlasting covenant of peace with the people" (37:26). This covenant was marked by integrity, justice, and care for all life. And a further mark of the covenant was that God was the sole security and life-force of the people. The Israelites, the People of God, were to be witnesses to all the world of the light of God's glory, of unity among all of creation, and witnesses to a life lived free from fear, slavery, insecurity, and war (Leviticus 26:3–16).

The Messiah

Isaiah describes the hope of the people, the Messiah, simply: "He will faithfully bring forth justice" (42:3). This Messiah would bring forth peace and he would be peace, and his coming would be a gift and a reward for faithfulness to the laws of God. Jesus becomes Shalom, a person dwelling with us who is the presence of God with his people. Jesus brings peace to the world and to its inhabitants. The night of his birth the angels sing: "Peace on earth to all of good will." Jesus' message is the making of peace, being peace to others.

Who is the greatest hero? One who changes an enemy into a friend.

The Bishops' Pastoral Letter on War and Peace, *The Challenge of Peace: God's Promise and Our Response*, notes some of the characteristics of Jesus' message, actions, and kingdom. They all have to do with peace.

Jesus announces the reign of God has come in him and is already among the people (Luke 17:20–21; 12:32). The peacemakers are called the children of God in the Sermon on the Mount (Matthew 5:3–10), and Jesus' call to conversion goes beyond the law to a new way of living in the spirit of God himself. The characteristics of this new way are mercy and forgiveness.

Jesus' message is one of love, a love that goes beyond family ties and bonds of friendship to reach out to even those who are enemies. This kind of love does not seek revenge, but is merciful in the face of threat and opposition.

The actions of Jesus and the gift of his Spirit make peace possible. And his message and his actions were considered dangerous in his time, leading to his death, a cruel and viciously inflicted death, a criminal's death (Galatians 3:13). And in all of his suffering, as in all of his life and ministry, Jesus refused to defend himself with force or with violence. He endured violence and cruelty so that God's love might be made fully manifest and so that the world might be reconciled to the One from whom it had become estranged. And his last words were words of forgiveness.

Jesus' Peace

After his resurrection, Jesus went to his disciples who were hiding, greeting them with, "Shalom! Peace be with you," repeated over and over again. But it is a "peace not as the world gives" (John 14:27). And Saint Paul describes Jesus' life, death, and resurrection as the reconciliation of all things to God (Romans 5:1–2; Colossians 1:20).

Jesus has shared with us his peace, his holiness, and his completeness of God's goodness, justice, and truth in a human being. We are called by Baptism to be "ministers of reconciliation" (2 Corinthians 5:19–20), people who would make visible the peace that God had established, through love and unity within their own communities.

Peace and Reconciliation

The gift of peace begins within and then extends outward; it is given as a gift. "A gift is not a gift until it has been given twice" is an old Indian saying, and it holds true especially for the gift of peace. Peace does not mean peace of mind, but peace in our relations with others, in thought, in speech, in mind, and in action. It means that people do not set themselves or their race or their nation up as their own goal or as a privileged position. It means that all peace is built on justice. Pope Paul VI said, "If you want peace, work for justice."

Peace within cannot stay inside or be hoarded. It must be expressed in forgiveness, mercy, and reconciliation. The word *reconciliation* means "to walk together again, as friends." It is a demanding action and a state of mind and heart. This kind of reconciliation is a building of tolerance, respect, and understanding in situations of conflict, and it never reduces conflict to "two sides," remembering that those "sides" are people.

For Christians, peace is seen as the mission of Jesus, to keep, maintain, and deepen peace between all people, as Jesus made peace between God his Father and us, his brothers and sisters.

The Sign of the Cross: Peace and Reconciliation

The last four Beatitudes look at the virtues and commandments to be merciful, to be singlehearted (pure), to make peace, and to suffer persecution for the sake of the Gospel. These are calls to live under the sign of the cross, the sign of power for those who live as disciples of Jesus. Jesus is the model of Christian life, and his actions and words brought him resistance and suffering. But he faced this opposition nonviolently, trusting in God and being steadfast in his love and forgiveness of all who turned against him. These last four Beatitudes ask us to be merciful as God has been merciful to us, forgiving and loving us. We are to look to God alone for power and authority, and we are to worship him alone, purely. And we are to do the work of God: make peace in the world. And if this causes us suffering, persecution, insults, or slander, then we are to rejoice for we are imitating Jesus in his life.

> *Peace does not mean peace of mind, but peace in our relations with others, in thought, in speech, in mind, and in action.*

We are made in the image and likeness of God, and, as Christians, this image is the sign of the cross. We stand between earth and sky, pointing to God, with arms outstretched, we reach for others. We are called to be the sign of peace, the sign of hope and reconciliation in the world. The sign of the cross, our own form as human beings, is the sign of the presence of God, the presence of peace for others to see and from which to take heart. It is the sign of salvation and of grace, and it is the way the world was meant to be.

WHAT ABOUT YOU?

1. What are words that describe the reality of peace?
2. Jesus Christ is our peace. How does Jesus bring peace to others in his life?
3. How do you reflect your belief in peace?
4. You are made in the sign of the cross. What does this sign mean for others?

SCRIPTURE ACTIVITY

What I Say to You

Read Matthew 5:21–26 on being angry and in need of reconciliation with others. Then answer the following questions.

1. What actions or feelings constitute anger?

2. What should you do before going to worship God?

3. How far do you have to go in trying to reconcile yourself to others?

4. If we offer our gift before being reconciled, what will happen to us?

5. From this reading, is God going to deal with us justly or mercifully?

SCRIPTURE ACTIVITY

Forgiveness and Peace

Read the following Scripture passages and write down what Jesus has to say about how we are to forgive one another and live in peace with one another.

SCRIPTURE	HOW WE ARE TO LIVE
Matthew 18:15–17	
Matthew 18:1–4	
Matthew 7:1–2	
Matthew 7:3–5	
Matthew 5:38–42	
Matthew 5:43–48	
Matthew 26:51–52	

GROUP ACTIVITY

Peace that the World Cannot Give

Part I

The Bishops' Peace Pastoral lists four kinds of peace. Write down some suggestions on how you, as a group, can encourage each kind of peace in your own lives.

1. Individual's sense of well-being or security

   _____

   _____

   _____

2. Cessation of armed hostility, producing an atmosphere in which nations can relate to one another and settle conflicts without resorting to the use of arms

   _____

   _____

   _____

3. A right relationship with God, which entails forgiveness, reconciliation, and union

   _____

   _____

   _____

4. An eschatological peace: a peace that is final and a full realization of God's salvation when all creation will be made whole

   _____

   _____

   _____

   _____

PART II

Until the fourth century, there was a tradition that no soldier could be baptized because his life-style was considered to be in direct opposition to Jesus' words of loving one's enemy, worshiping God alone, and not harming others. Today, at age eighteen, each young man is required to register for the military draft.

What do you think Jesus would have to say about each of the following actions that are sometimes ordered in times of war?

Bombing of civilian populations:

Torture to get information:

Lying and covering up for someone's actions:

Using a nuclear weapon:

Considering everyone in a place "the enemy" because suspected enemies are in the area:

In your own words, what does Jesus have to say about war?

10 Living in Christ Jesus

PREPARATION PAGE

Where Am I Now?

1. What do you think is the most difficult moral imperative that Christ gave his disciples?

2. How are you actively trying to be a disciple of Jesus Christ now?

3. Who is a person alive in the world today that you think is a disciple of Christ? What does this person do to proclaim his or her belief in Jesus' values and morals?

READING ACTIVITY

A Christian Soap Opera

Once upon a time there were two friends, John and Anna. They had grown up together, gone to school and knew each others' families for as long as they could remember. During their last year of high school, they realized that they had fallen in love with each other and they were thinking of getting married. They decided over Christmas vacation that they would fix their schedules so that they could borrow a friend's cabin in the mountains, and move in together for two weeks. At the end of that time, they were pretty sure they'd know if they wanted to commit themselves to marriage.

Everything went as planned. Anna came home and celebrated the holidays with her family. She spent some time with John but nothing out of the ordinary. Then she told her parents she was going back to school early. John left before she did and went up to the cabin to fix up the place, get the food, and wait for her to arrive.

The night before Anna left to go to the cabin, she received a phone call. It was from a neighbor near the cabin in the mountains where John was staying. There had been an accident and the bridge was out over the river—the only way into the cabin. John had been on the bridge when it collapsed. He was hurt, in a lot of pain, and alone. He really needed her to get up there fast, however she could. Anna arrived in the small fishing village downriver from the cabin, and she began to inquire about a boat up to the house.

She was approached by a young man, Steve, who owned a boat and would ferry the mail and passengers up and down the river. He offered to take her. Anna offered to pay him. Steve laughed and said, "No, I don't need the money. But I tell you what—you sleep with me tonight and I'll take you wherever you want to go tomorrow morning early." She was floored and refused. She couldn't do that. She loved John. After all, this whole trip was to see if she and John wanted to get married. She was back where she started. Anna wandered around the town the rest of the afternoon and no one seemed to care.

She met a man named Ivan, and she told him that this guy Steve had offered to take her up river, but that he wanted sex. Ivan listened. He always did. He knew everything about everybody. He even knew that Steve had VD. But he didn't say anything to Anna about that. All he said was, "Honey, the way I see it, you've got a decision to make. It's getting late. Leave me alone."

Anna was getting nervous and frightened. She wondered how John was: alone and hurt in the cabin, waiting for her. How was she going to get there? She walked around and thought about Steve's option. How could she? But John needed her. She had to get to him and this seemed the only way. Finally around nightfall, she went back to the deli and found Steve. She told him: "I'm desperate to get up the river to my friend. I'll pay your price. Let's go."

Early the next morning, Steve ferried up the river and dropped Anna at the small dock near the cabin. John was overjoyed to see her. They spent two beautiful weeks together, and they knew long before it was over that they loved each other and wanted to get married. Anna meant to tell John how she had gotten to him, but she just kept putting it off. In the rush of work and study and preparations for the wedding, Anna never told him about Steve.

But the memory of what she had done and what had happened kept eating away at Anna. She knew she had to tell John what happened. It was a few months after their first anniversary and she finally got up her courage and decided to tell him. She got home early, cleaned the house, made his favorite dinner, and dressed up. She met him at the door and they sat in the living room with a glass of wine. She began by kissing him and telling him she loved him. And then she said she had something to tell him but she was afraid. He held her and told her he loved her and that she could tell him anything. She was his wife, his friend and love; he trusted her. Back and forth it went over another glass of wine and finally, Anna blurted it out.

John was stunned. He just looked at her in disbelief and silence as it dawned on him what she had said. He had a terrible temper, and when he finally spoke, he yelled. He called her every name in the book. Anna began to cry hysterically and yell back at him, even though she knew that wouldn't help. The fight went on and on. John hit her and punched her around. She ran out of the house, crying.

Anna knocked on the door of her friend Dick's house. Dick opened the door and couldn't believe what he saw. Anna looked terrible—the tears, a blackened eye, and the torn dress. She was obviously distraught. This time, in between sobs, she told him the story: what John had done to her and why he had hit her. As Dick listened, he got angry. And the more she cried and talked, the angrier and more upset he became. Then he decided to go see John and tell him a thing or two.

John opened the door expecting to see Anna. He was still angry, but he was beginning to calm down and think about things. However, seeing Dick at the door just made him angry all over again. John didn't like others interfering in his personal life, and he certainly didn't like this guy butting in. Before they knew what was happening, they were throwing punches at each other. The door was open when Anna returned and the house was a mess. The fight was still going on, and both Dick and John looked horrible. Anna was soon screaming again—this time to stop. But the two men barely heard her. Just then, Dick grabbed the poker from the fireplace and hit John in the head. John hit the floor, lifeless. In an instant, Anna was beside him. Dick stood there with the poker in his hand.

THINK IT OVER

1. Who do you think did the worst thing wrong? Why?
2. Who do you think was the best Christian in the story? Why did you choose him or her?
3. What was the most important Christian value that was broken? What would you have done differently to protect and defend that value?

STUDY

What Pleases the Lord

Morality, right living and choosing, following Jesus as a disciple—all these things are what please the Lord. We are disciples of Jesus and so we try to live out in our lives the values and message of God that is revealed in Jesus Christ. The choice to do this and the actions that are the effects of these choices are not always easy to practice. Sometimes we choose rightly; other times we fail, out of ignorance or fear or pressure or laziness or anger. We are sometimes "Yes" to God in our lives, and sometimes we are just as loudly "No" to his word and his invitation. But Saint Paul tells us that Jesus was "always Yes to God." And he is always "Yes" to us, whether we fail him or live up to his standards and seek to grow in his holiness and way of living.

Morality, right living and choosing, following Jesus as a disciple—all these things are what please the Lord.

Jesus Is the Rule

We have looked at and studied the laws and commandments of the Old Testament as well as the commandments of love and the Beatitudes in the New Testament, the new covenant we have with God in Jesus. But in reality there is only one rule, one law—and that is Jesus. Jesus Christ, our Master and Teacher, the One we follow, is the only rule. Each time that we choose to imitate him, we learn more about what it means to be a Christian, a Christ-bearer. And there is always more to learn. We must always look to Jesus and see what he says, what he does, and what he calls us to do and be. And then we must try to imitate him.

In Baptism, we are given the Spirit of Jesus, to help us discern what is right and what we are supposed to do. It is the same Spirit that encourages us and gives us grace to act as we know we should in the face of fear or want or outside pressures. And the Spirit forgives us and calls us back to Christ, assuring us of forgiveness and showing us what we should do to change what we did before. The Christian life, the living out of Christian morality, is a lifetime endeavor.

The Church as Moral Teacher

Each of us chooses to follow Jesus as Lord and to be his disciple. But while we must all make individual and personal choices in our lifetime and vocation, we are also baptized in his community, his Church. The Church is the followers of Jesus banded together under his Spirit, trying to live the commandments of love and justice and forgiveness in every generation and in every place. We all need help from our friends, and our best friends are our friends in the Spirit, who struggle with us to act in imitation of Jesus. The Spirit teaches us to pray and to understand what is demanded in certain situations, and the Spirit helps us to put our belief into practice.

The Spirit of Jesus is our first teacher. But we have another teacher: the Church. Jesus sent the Spirit to his followers after his resurrection so that we would always be reminded of what he said and did, called to a life lived in his power. John tells us of Jesus' words at the Last Supper with his friends. He describes the work of the Spirit and what he will do for us:

> Whoever loves me will keep my word, and my Father will love him, and we will come to him and make our dwelling with him. Whoever does not love me does not keep my words; yet the word you hear is not mine but that of the Father who sent me.
> I have told you this while I am still with you. The Advocate, the holy Spirit that the Father will send in my name, will teach you everything and remind you of all that I told you.
> John 14:23–26

> It is better for you that I go. For if I do not go, the Advocate will not come to you. But if I go, I will send him to you. And when he comes he will convict the world in regard to sin and righteousness and condemnation. . . . But when he comes, the Spirit of truth, he will guide you to all truth.
> John 16:7–8, 13

This gift of the Spirit is shared with us in Baptism, and it is there to help us live up to our promises. Our promises are open-ended, not specific. "Do you reject sin so as to live in the freedom of God's children? Do you reject the glamor of evil and refuse to be mastered by sin? Do you reject Satan, father of sin and prince of darkness?" We turn from sin and evil toward Jesus Christ the Lord, who enlightens us and shows us the way to the Father.

But the gift of the Spirit is also shared with the Church community, especially the bishops and teachers of the faith. They are charged with reminding the whole community of our promises and the more specific choices that our baptismal promises protect. They uphold the highest ideals that Jesus presented to us, and they call us to try and live up to them. Even if we fail or struggle in certain situations, we are reminded of them and they are kept before us as goals.

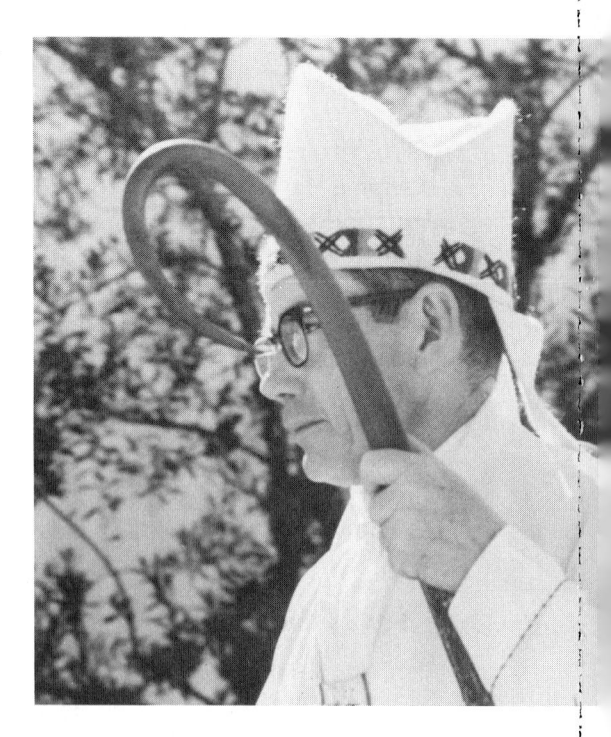

We turn from sin and evil toward Jesus Christ the Lord, who enlightens us and shows us the way to the Father.

Ideals and Moral Imperatives

Jesus' ideals have been presented here. These are the beliefs of the Church. And it is the work of the Church to protect those ideals from anyone or anything that would water them down or change them. In defending Jesus' principles and high standards of living, the Church can sometimes sound sharp or judgmental or condemning, but it is only trying to make clear the basic, underlying principles of Jesus' way, truth, and life. The Church is people, like us, and although it makes mistakes in how it may present teachings or in how it may react to situations, that does not mean that its teaching is wrong.

The core of Jesus' message is found in the Scriptures and in the tradition of the Church. Its teaching over the last two thousand years rounds out and makes more specific how believers have interpreted those teachings and tried to live up to them in their own lives. Sometimes, as with the saints and some of the people we have read about in this book, they have opted to die for their beliefs. Individuals have the Spirit that helps them to discern what is necessary for them to live up to Jesus' teaching, and, together with the same Spirit given to the Church universal, people grow in their understanding of what it means to follow Jesus Christ in each generation.

Teachings can be unclear, personally hard to live up to, or confusing. But there are certain rules of thumb for deciding what to do in a given situation. Whatever calls us to greater love and forgiveness of other people overrules all other issues. Compassion, love, justice,

Jesus came to save us and to remind us of why we were created and how we can live with grace and freedom.

truth, and how that is shared with people come first. Jesus came to save us and to remind us of why we were created and how we can live with grace and freedom. It is people and their life and hope that come first. Ideals and laws are always found in their truest meanings in people. The laws, the commandments, are like a skeleton, bones that hold a body upright. But the community, the Church, puts flesh and blood and sinew on the skeleton. And the Spirit gives it life, breath, and the possibility for living out in reality the words of the law and the commandments.

You Aren't Lost; You Just Need Directions

There is a story told in the mountains of Maine and Vermont about a traveler who found himself on the wrong road and thought he was hopelessly lost. He drove into a village and stopped the first person he saw. "Friend," he said, "I'm lost. Can you help me out?" The villager looked at him for a long moment and then said, "You see the name of the village on the sign on the way in here?" "Sure," the man in the car answered. "Well then, you aren't lost. You know *where* you are." Then the villager said, "You know where you want to be? "Sure," the motorist again answered, and he told the man his destination. Again, the villager looked at him a long time and finally said, "You aren't lost—you just need directions."

This story, as simple a it is, tells us something we need to remember. Often, we *know* what we should do, or we know the rules, the laws, and the commandments, and we even know where we want to be as followers of Jesus, but we get turned around or confused or we get involved in other things or hang around with others who think differently than we do or we get lazy and disoriented—and we think we're lost. But we're not lost; we just need directions. The Church is there to provide the directions, to tell us how to get where we want to go by the most direct and easily accessible route.

The Way of the Cross

The most direct way, however, is not always the easiest. The way of Jesus led to Jerusalem, the way of the cross, and eventually his death, and then resurrection and glory. We are told in the Gospels that, at one point in his life and his preaching, Jesus "set his face toward Jerusalem." And when he told his followers where they were going and what was going to happen to him, they didn't like it. The story is told in Mark's Gospel:

> [Jesus] began to teach them that the Son of Man must suffer greatly and be rejected by the elders, the chief priests, and the scribes, and be killed, and rise after three days. He spoke this openly. Then Peter took him aside and began to rebuke him. At this he turned around and, looking as his disciples, rebuked Peter and said, "Get behind me, Satan. You are thinking not as God does, but as human beings do."
>
> Mark 8:31–33

It seems that Jesus didn't always get support or help from his friends. He had to deal with their rejection of him as well as with his own choices to be obedient to his Father's will. It is immediately following this incident in the Gospel that Jesus makes very plain and clear what following him might mean:

> He summoned the crowd with his disciples and said to them, "Whoever wishes to come after me must deny himself, take up his cross, and follow me. For whoever wishes to save his life will lose it, but whoever loses his life for my sake and that of the gospel will save it. What profit is there for one to gain the whole world and forfeit his life? What could one give in exchange for his life? Whoever is ashamed of me and my doctrine in this faithless and sinful generation, the Son of Man will be ashamed of when he comes in his Father's glory with the holy angels."
>
> Mark 8:34–38

Jesus' way is the way of the cross, the way of suffering and death, but it is the way that leads to life; life everlasting and abundant life—even here. We make our moral decisions as Christians because Jesus made them first and lived them out so that we could see the life, goodness, justice, and truth that came forth from them.

It is Christ's love, his forgiveness, his becoming one with us in life and death, and the gift of resurrection that he shares with us that gives us the power and the possibility of living as he does. God's strength is shared with his friends and children. We always fail, but we always have the word of God forgiving us and loving us, the Spirit of God encouraging us and helping to change us, and the community of believers that can pray for and with us and help us to be faithful to what we say we believe.

Where Are You Now?

In the story of the Garden of Eden, when Adam and Eve sin, God comes after them, and calls out to Adam: "Where are you?" God is all-knowing; why does he ask where Adam is? This question was once asked of a rabbi who was persecuted and imprisoned. His captors wanted to trip him up, and they said: "You believe that your God is omniscient and knows all wisdom. How come your God had to ask and go looking for Adam after he had sinned?" The rabbi answered with another question: "Do you know that we believe that the Scriptures are eternal so that every generation and every man and woman is included in them?" "Oh," his jailer said, "what does that mean?" "It means," said the rabbi, "that in every era God calls out to every man and woman at each stage of their life and puts the question to them: 'Where are you? Where do you stand *now*? So many years of your life have passed, how far have you gotten in worshiping me and living up to my commandments?' For instance, right now, God is saying to me, 'You are forty-six years old, how far along are you now?'" The story says that the rabbi had chosen the age of the jailer, and the question hit him hard enough to make him examine his own life.

This is the question God asks each of us at every moment of our life. He wants to know where each of us stands right now, and each of us has to answer God. We answer with more than words: we answer with our desires and our efforts and our actions. And God sees and knows all, and God is with us in all our judgments and responses. Even when we fail, he asks again, "Where are you now?," and adds, "I am with you still." This is our hope as Christians.

WHAT ABOUT YOU?

1. Where are you now in your commitment to Jesus' commandments?
2. What is hard and what is good about following Jesus' way, even when it becomes the way of the cross?
3. How can the Church help you to live up to your belief and promises at baptism?
4. How can you help the Church to live up to the teachings of Jesus?

SCRIPTURE ACTIVITY

How Jesus Makes a Hard Moral Decision

Read Luke's account of Jesus praying and deciding to face his accusers in the Garden of Gethsemane on the night he was betrayed. It is found in Luke 22:39–46. Think about how Jesus must have felt and how he prayed. Then answer the following questions for yourself:

1. Jesus told his disciples to pray so they wouldn't fall into temptation and then they fell asleep. What kind of situations in your life do you need to pray before so that you don't fall into temptation?

2. The decision that Jesus had to reach was so difficult that it made him physically ill, and he began to sweat blood. When you have to make a hard decision, how does your body react?

3. When Jesus is finished praying he comes back to his disciples and says: "Wake up!" What do you think he meant when he said this?

4. Jesus prayed on the ground and three times in the words: "Father, if it is your will, take this cup from me; yet not my will but yours be done." What does this prayer tell you about Jesus and how he decided what to do?

SCRIPTURE ACTIVITY

You Always Get Another Chance

Read the story of the two thieves crucified with Jesus. It is found in Luke 23:39–43. This is the last conversation Jesus has with people before he dies. Answer these questions in light of what Jesus thought was important.

1. The "good" thief asks Jesus to remember him when he comes into his kingdom. Why do you think he's referred to as a "good" thief, after all his actions make him a sinner and someone who broke the law?

   _____

   _____

2. Jesus *assures* him that he has a place and will share life with him that very day. What do Jesus' words say about how he reacts to us if we ask him to remember us?

   _____

   _____

   _____

3. One of the last things Jesus does is give his kingdom away to someone who didn't "deserve" it. What are some of the things you'd like to do as your last things?

   _____

   _____

   _____

4. If you were to die tonight how would you feel about your life up to now? Write a prayer to Jesus and tell him what you want to do and how you'd like to live.

   _____

   _____

   _____

GROUP ACTIVITY

Where Do You Stand Now?

Reread the Christian Soap Opera story in the Reading Activity. Then answer the following questions:

1. Who do you think did the worst thing wrong and why?

   _____

   _____

   _____

   _____

   _____

   _____

   _____

2. Look at each person and list the civil laws they broke.

   Anna _____

   John _____

   Ivan _____

   Steve _____

   Dick _____

3. What sins or failures in morality did each commit?

   Anna _____

   John _____

   Ivan _____

   Steve _____

   Dick _____

4. What should/could each of the characters have done differently—more in line with right living and Christian moral decision making?

   Anna _____

   John _____

   Ivan _____

   Steve _____

   Dick _____

5. Write what you think Jesus would have said to each character. (Keep in mind Jesus' own experiences with his own disciples, friends, and the people he encountered.)

   Anna _____

   John _____

   Ivan _____

   Steve _____

   Dick _____

6. Think of one line from the Gospels that reveals Jesus' attitude toward his disciples who are both sinners and his friends. Pick a line that says something about where you are in relationship to Jesus right now. Write it out below with a short prayer for help to the Spirit of Jesus in living up to and beyond that line.

   The Scripture Line: _____

   The Prayer: _____

   _____

   _____

   _____

   _____

   _____